R...
A...
Because Life Doesn't Come with an Instruction Manual

"Eight word self-affirmations, such as 'I am in charge of my personal happiness,' and New Age esoteric aphorisms may work for some people, but not everyone.

In A Year of Encouragements, Randy Mazie offers observations about himself in an appealingly-quirky style, and in listening in on his self-reflections, we are reminded of how we can constructively and supportively deal with our own imperfections in a less than perfect world."

—*Sheldon "Shel" Malett, Psychologist, Ph.D.*

"We all need some encouragement from time to time. Mr. Mazie's book provides a daily dose of encouragement that helps keep me from getting overwhelmed by life's twists and turns."

—*Mark Donahue, Teacher*

"I very much enjoyed this thoughtful collection of encouraging ideas put together by Mr. Mazie from his own life experiences.

The book lays out encouragements for coping with life and relationships in a thoughtful and spiritual way. An excellent read for anyone who has gone through or is still going through rough periods in their life."

—*David W. Heath, Managing Partner, OnTrack Performance Tools*

More Praise for *A Year of Encouragements*

"Through his stunning candor and powerful examples, Mr. Mazie shows us how he works toward a more balanced, satisfying life through the process of self-reflection, insight, and readjustment.

He encourages us to use our own power of thought to modify how we react to the everyday challenges of life—fear, anger, depression, insecurity, stress—so that we too can approach each day with optimism and techniques to make it better.

This book is valuable for anyone seeking personal growth or for professionals facilitating growth in others. I've already started!"

—*Mimi Cooperman Schuurmans, Social Worker, MSW*

"*A Year of Encouragements* is written with great clarity, wisdom, and humor.

Randy Mazie offers quick, easy-to-read, and thought-provoking daily introspections which encourage and help guide readers to successfully navigate through life's everyday dilemmas.

It worked for me!"

—*E. R. Marsden, Writer*

"The beauty of *A Year of Encouragements* is that it never comes across as either preachy or cliché.

The more I read it, the more I feel like a wise, trusted and often funny old friend was simply expressing his thoughts as we sit on the back porch.

Quite honestly, it was impossible to just read one page daily. I found myself reading several pages at a time and then the following day, going back to the one I was supposed to read . . . and then I'd read some more.

Brilliant yet simplistic. Meaningful and witty. I highly recommend this book."

—*Randy Levin, Educational Consultant (NYC)*

A Year of Encouragements

Because
Life Doesn't Come with an Instruction Manual

Randy Mazie

A Year of Encouragements Press, LLC

A Year of Encouragements
Because Life Doesn't Come with an Instruction Manual
Randy Mazie
ISBN 979-8-9850209-0-8 (male cover); 979-8-9850209-1-5 (female cover)

Published by
A Year of Encouragements Press, LLC
315 Young Harris St., #2343
Blairsville, GA 30514
www.AYearOfEncouragements.com
mail@AYearOfEncouragements.com

Please visit our website for more information about this and other books, app information, gift items, order links, and other FAQs.

Cover Design: Robin Locke Monda
Interior Design and Typesetting: Saul Bottcher, IndieBookLauncher.com

The body text of this book is set in Adobe Caslon.

Notice of Rights
Copyright 2021 Randy Mazie, all rights reserved. No part of this book may be used or reproduced in any manner without written permission, except in the case of brief references ascribed to or made by noted historical figures or celebrities which are in the public domain. For further information, contact the publisher at the above address.

Also Available
E-book edition (male cover), ISBN 979-8-9850209-2-2
E-book edition (female cover), ISBN 979-8-9850209-3-9

CONTENTS

Preface 9
Intro to My Year of Encouragements 11

Welcome to My World... 13
Learning to Take it Easy 65
Tools, Tools, and More Tools.. 109
Overcoming Adversity.. 159
Always Seeking Something 209
Practice, Practice, Practice 259
Humor, Comfort, and Trust 309

Reference Research... 390
Acknowledgments 392
About the Author.. 394
Have You Ever Been Encouraged? 396

*This book is dedicated to my wife, Debbie,
who I love, and has loved me and has stood by me,
encouraging me every step of the way—
and to my four children who I love dearly:
Ara, Elyse, Kylie, and Gabe.*

Preface

Life doesn't come with an instruction manual.

But it's good that it doesn't because most instruction manuals take forever to read, and most people don't have the time or interest to read the whole thing anyway.

A Year of Encouragements was written with this in mind.

Social media seems to dominate our lives today. We're used to Texting, Tweeting, Instagram, FB, TikTok, and the like. If we don't "get something" right away, then we don't usually want to spend much more time on it. Our attention spans are a lot shorter.

These writings are intended to provide basic ideas about how to cope with life. But it does it in a sort of "social media" format. Quick, short, and simple messages.

It does not provide instructions. It can't because there is no instruction manual. It does, however, provide encouragements, suggestions, and tools that can help make decisions on how to live life in the most comfortable and best ways possible for each of us.

It also doesn't provide answers. It is written to encourage each of us to find our own. However, many of these encouragements are similar in nature as I have found that "repetition is both the mother of change as well as consistency."

What I need, and I hope that if you are seeking the same things that this will provide it for you too, is the comfort that I want to have in living life, the help I need to change in order to achieve that, and the practice I need to keep my life in balance and as consistent as it possibly can be.

Life is always in flux, and it's me who needs to adapt to it, but the way that I adapt can be dependable and relatively easily practiced. That's what A Year of Encouragements is all about.

Consider yourself encouraged.

Welcome.

Intro to A Year of Encouragements

As a way of introducing myself and what this is all about, I want to let you know that there have been many days in my life when I have been frustrated, down, fearful, and angry.

Times when I was scared. Not knowing what to do.

I needed help, but I was afraid to ask.

Eventually, I sought help from counselors, twelve step programs, hypnotists, friends, and family.

But when the help ended, I realized I still needed a consistent message in my life. I needed to be reminded of the tools that worked and to practice them every day.

You see, I forget.

When things get really good or don't go my way, I lose perspective.

Life doesn't come with instructions. So, I continue to need help. I need tools to use regularly.

It's how I keep my life relatively in balance.

I use daily encouragements and I practice.

Welcome to My World

No Pollyanna Here

I don't believe that I will ever be perfectly happy.

Nor do I believe that I will be happy all the time.

I am no Pollyanna.

In fact, I'm uncomfortable with people who tell me to be happy or who act as if they are happy all the time.

I have frustrating days. Sad days. Days of remembering loved ones who are no longer around. I get disappointed. I get upset. And so on.

But every day is an opportunity to encourage myself to be as supportive of those I care about as I can be.

That means more to me than being happy or being told to be happy.

I Need Reminders

I tend to worry too much, overdo things, get hurt too easily, withdraw from situations, obsess, and plot, at times, about how I'm going to "get back at someone"—and as a result, some days, I don't even want to get out of bed.

I need reminders.

Reminders to keep everything as simple as possible.

Encouragement to help me sort things through.

Gentle nudges in the morning to help me consider where and how to start.

For instance, I need reminding that I don't have to take on the entire day first thing in the morning.

I only need to take a few small first steps.

Like, just get out of bed and get the coffee going.

I can handle that.

The Hardest Thing is to Remember

The hardest thing that I have had to learn about myself is what my limits are.

What I can and cannot do.

But what's even harder is to remember them.

You see, once I start to feel good and everything is going well, I forget them.

I tend to overdo things and stretch myself way too thin.

Before I know it, I'm back in a state of anxiety, depression, or self-pity.

It's my memory I have to work on.

Best to remind myself of that every day.

Principles

I can take myself way too seriously when I stand on my principles.

I can be inflexible: refusing to listen to someone else, entertain a change, or consider that I could be wrong.

Really?

What makes me so right?

In the spirit of lighthearted people like Groucho Marx, Yogi Berra, and Mark Twain, I've learned to lighten up a little by using humorous expressions, like:

- When I get carried away by principles, I usually don't like the trip, and
- If I stand on my principles, it makes it that much harder to reach them.

I need principles, but sometimes I hold on to them so tightly that I can bend myself and others out of shape.

I need to be open-minded, and I like the idea that if I develop enough principles, I can use the ones that best work for me in any given situation.

I Need Time for Me Before I Do Anything Else

Each morning, when I first wake up, I need "me" time.

Time for me:

- before the kids wake up, begin to squabble, and need to be cared for.
- before my significant other starts telling me their agenda for the day.
- before my brain kicks into gear worrying about everything I have to do.

I sit up straight, stretch, and breathe.

I remember how grateful I am for what I have.

I read some spiritual literature.

I spend a few minutes thinking about what I'd like to accomplish today or maybe only in the next few minutes—but mostly, how important it is to pace myself, so I don't get bent out of shape.

I remind myself to take my time. I'm no good to anyone if I'm rushing and not taking care of "me" first.

See all those "I's"? That's because it is "me" time.

Stubbornly Believing That Only I Know What's Right

I get crazy stubbornly arguing with someone over some issue. And I insist I know better.

Maybe I do, but I make both of us miserable because of it.

It helps when I entertain the idea that you have as much right to your opinion as I do.

(Even if you are wrong!)

Or when I concede that some part of what you are saying might be true.

(I do this grudgingly.)

And if I am really honest, maybe only part of what I'm saying is true too.

Maybe I don't know everything.

(That can't be true, can it?)

Ultimately, whoever, whatever, is right or wrong—so what?

To the degree that I stubbornly argue about it, I make both of us unhappy.

Even more sad is the fact that I can waste my entire day arguing with you in my head.

Five Easy Minutes

It didn't take a lot of effort or time to see improvements in my life.

I once read that 10-15 minutes a day of exercise, just enough to break a sweat, can improve my overall health. So, I began to think, what-the-heck, anyone can do that.

In fact, I read that I could even do 7 minutes in the morning and 7 minutes in the evening, and that would work too.

Then I thought that maybe I could do the same with my spiritual life. And I found that it even takes less time than that.

All I need is five minutes in the morning over a cup of coffee or tea, reading some words of encouragement, a moment or two of reflection, and a reminder of how grateful I am for what I have—and I am off and running towards a better and usually more uplifting day ahead.

Notice I didn't say "happy."

Life still happens.

A Few Extra Minutes

Some days I don't feel like taking time to encourage myself.

It just feels like too much effort.

But then I think about how irritable I can get. How anxious or how disappointed I can feel—and then I think how just a few minutes of encouragement right now might not be too much effort at all.

In fact, it might just be the best thing for me.

And then I think, maybe if I do a few extra minutes, sort of as an insurance policy, I might even make it a great day.

I Try to Remind Myself

As I go through the day, beyond the time I take each morning to encourage myself, I try to remind myself how grateful I am for what I have.

I try to remind myself that *I am* enjoying this day.

I try to remind myself to have fun. To make this day and what I'm doing fun.

I try to remind myself that I'm doing my best—or at least doing as much as I need to do or can do.

I try to remind myself that everybody else is trying too.

I try to be as helpful to others as I can.

I try to encourage others, reminding them that they are doing the *best they can* too.

I like to take this encouragement with me, in my pocket, so I can remember.

Shakespeare Once Wrote

Shakespeare wrote in Hamlet, "This above all: to thine own self be true..."

Each morning, to the best of my ability, I take time to think about what I really want.

But more importantly, I need to consider what's really good for me.

Because what I really want is not necessarily what's really good for me.

For instance, I often want people to approve of me and what I'm doing.

But if I stop and think about it, trying to get people's approval may not be in my best interest.

Especially if I feel I have to give up what might be in my best interest——just to gain their approval.

I need to pursue what's really good for me first.

Then, everything else might fall into place.

Everything Could Be as it Should Be

I've heard this a thousand times. And sometimes it makes me want to puke:

Everything is as it should be.

You know: birds fly, flowers sprout, fish swim. The sun comes up every day.

All very true.

But I *have* to work at making everything the way it should be.

You see, I don't think it happens on its own.

I have to work at not letting you, or me, get in the way.

Mostly me.

To have everything as it should be, I have to not step on my own toes.

I'm going to *try not to do that* today.

Today Before I Get Myself Bent Out of Shape

Today

- before I get myself bent out of shape over something,
- before I go off on a rant,
- before I tell you how wrong you are,
- before I sit down and gloat over your stupidity,
- before I start telling other people what you did and how wrong it was,
- before I get myself exhausted and worried that now everyone is upset with me,
- before I obsess about how that person I told off is going to try to get even,
- before I start feeling anxious about everything,
- before I run away, withdraw, call in sick, or stay in bed

I just need to ask myself one little question *before* I get started:

Is it really worth making myself and everyone around me crazy?

Beginning to See a Change

As each day goes by, some good and others still difficult, I'm beginning to see changes.

Things are getting a little easier.

When I look back at what it used to be like, I can see light at the end of the tunnel.

I'm beginning to think about talking with others about this, what changes have happened, and maybe encourage someone else too.

It would be nice to talk with someone else who's having a hard time and tell them what it was like and what I'm doing differently now.

Who knows? It might help them. It will certainly help me.

It's nice to begin thinking beyond myself and maybe helping someone else—as shaky as I might still be.

But it is getting better.

Their Outsides and My Insides

When I see someone else who seems to handle adversity calmly, I wonder what's up with that person?

I get jealous and resentful.

What makes them so perfect?

But now I think: Who cares! I can't compare how I feel inside with someone else's outside.

Who knows how they *really* feel?

More importantly, I need to concern myself with my own feelings and *what I want to do* about them.

I've heard it said, "It's an inside job."

So, what's really important to me? How is this affecting me? What can I do about it?

Should I get involved? Walk away? Deal with it later?

Can I step back for a moment, breathe, and take time to decide how I want to proceed?

It's about me and my life.

It's not about someone else.

More About Their Outsides and My Insides

Someone once told me that when I see someone else reacting to adversity calmly, what I don't know is the time that person may have spent training him or herself to react that way.

Everyone reacts inwardly to adverse situations.

People who we perceive as being so calm have disciplined themselves to react that way.

They practiced being calm. And it took a lot of training. Nobody is born reacting that way.

That same person said to me that I was learning to remain calm myself.

I was training myself to recognize what I was feeling but not immediately act on it.

Calm people might smile, and think, "I'll sort this out later. It's not so important that I have to get myself upset and everyone else around me too."

It's no different from what I'm trying to teach myself to do today.

With practice, it gets easier.

It's All Good

I've heard the expression used "It's all good."

And I've begun to use that expression myself.

But when I say, "It's all good" what I'm really saying is "I'm grateful."

It lifts my spirits and helps to refocus me when I'm distressed.

"It's all good."

What I'm really doing is reminding myself to be grateful for what I have.

Grateful for the place I live in, my work, how I get around, my significant other and family, friends, and what I enjoy in life.

Grateful because things could be worse.

Some days I can only muster up enough energy to be grateful for having the basics: two hands, two legs, the ability to see, hear, smell, or just make myself a cup of damn coffee.

Those times I just grit my teeth and say, "It's all good," even if I don't mean it.

Who's in Charge?

I read this a while back and it stuck with me, helping me at times to relax and let things go.

If there is a God, a spirit of the universe, or some natural force holding everything together, I like to imagine it saying, or in today's world maybe even texting, something like this to me:

> *"Hi.*
> *Just want to let you that I'm here.*
> *I'm in charge of everything, and I can help you with all your problems today.*
> *Just wanted to let you know that I've got your back.*
> *You can just relax and chill, if you'd like.*
> *I don't need any help. At least not today.*
> *Have a good one."*

How's that for a perspective? Try repeating that several times over.

When I Get Quiet

When I take a few minutes in the morning to get quiet, I can usually hear this soft voice inside of me.

Sometimes it uses words, but just as often it is just a hum, a sense, something that I feel.

I breathe in and out and listen for it.

It relaxes me, it tells me it's all okay, and makes me feel whole or complete.

I feel connected to the world and I feel at peace. Tranquil and at ease.

I like taking a few minutes in the morning to do this.

Starts my day off nicely.

Plus, I've learned I can do this for a few minutes throughout the day if I want to.

Something Worth Considering

Today I try to make time to look around me and appreciate the natural greatness of the world: the warmth of the sun, the green-leafed trees, the expanse of skies that seemingly go on forever.

I wonder how all this came to be?

I certainly had nothing to do with it.

At times I can hear that small voice inside of me saying, "Be grateful that there is something so powerful that could create all this."

Amazing, I think.

And all I need to do is to enjoy it.

Appreciate it. And be grateful.

Will I allow myself to do that today?

Or do I still have to hold on tightly, trying to make everything be the way I want it to be?

My Insistence on Being Right

Sometimes when I'm discussing something with someone, I get pretty heated.

I don't understand how someone can actually believe what they're saying.

I think, "Don't they realize how wrong they are? How wrong that is?"

My insistence on being right can get in my way.

I get too worked up. I can obsess over it.

I can affect others with my bad mood.

But, when I stop and reflect on it, how important is it?

Why affect myself and others like I do?

Why do I need to prove I'm right?

Isn't just knowing what I believe in good enough for me?

And maybe what's right for someone else is simply that.

It's right for them.

How about I let it just end there?

Tools for Settling Down

There are many tools that I use to settle down. Here are some:

I sit up straight, concentrate on my breathing, repeat a phrase in my mind, or quietly chant something to myself.

Sometimes I repeat gibberish like "Shushenpadmeladeeahhh." It may sound silly but by using gibberish I can't focus on what's upsetting me.

Other times I repeat phrases like "All is well today. All is good." I breathe in saying "All is well today" and I breathe out saying "All is good."

Sometimes I go for a walk and say these phrases as I walk.

Being outside in the fresh air helps.

Music helps. Something soothing, with or without words.

Other times I imagine myself someplace that makes me feel better, like the mountains or the beach.

I have to practice settling myself down. Different things work at different times. Not everything works every time.

Listening to Others

I've realized that sometimes I really don't listen to what other people are saying.

I'm already deciding how I feel while they're talking, and then only wanting to convince them of why they are wrong or what my experience is and what they need to do.

I realize now how important it is to listen to what others have to say. To understand how they have arrived at their point of view.

I realize how important it is to ask questions. To see if even some part of what they're saying makes sense to me.

Maybe I can learn something new. Maybe see something differently than I already do.

Who knows, I might change and end up enjoying life more.

More Listening to Others

I've learned that I am never diminished by hearing what someone else has to say.

I may not always like what I hear, but I can, at least, try to understand what they're telling me. Listen to what caused them to feel the way they feel or believe what they believe.

Ultimately, I may not understand or appreciate their point of view, but I remind myself it's their experience and their point of view. It doesn't diminish mine.

I try not to "trap them in their words" or challenge them.

I only put someone on the defensive when I do that, and most likely they'll become angry or hurt in response.

If I'm getting upset, I just thank the person for sharing and politely end the conversation.

Later, when I'm calmer, I try to process what I've heard and put myself in their shoes a little more.

Avoiding Toxic People

While I find it's important to listen to people and try not to be quick to judge or allow my negative reactions to affect a conversation, there are people I find to be overly negative, very aggressive, and what I consider to be "toxic."

It's taken me a long time to allow myself to realize that there are people like this. People who are detrimental and who I need to stay away from.

It's been difficult coming to terms with this. I always wanted everyone to like me and believed that everybody was good.

Today I realize this isn't so and I avoid these people.

My life has become so much better. I'm no longer deeply affected by them.

But I also try to remember that when I go overboard, refuse to listen, get upset, argue, or say derogatory things to someone, I will be perceived as toxic too.

When I Become Conflicted

When I'm upset, it's generally because I feel threatened.

I'm feeling hurt, angry, or fearful—and then I shy away or try to retaliate.

I've come to realize that when I only focus on these feelings, I'm not helping myself or the situation.

What I need to do is reflect on what's bothering me.

It's usually because somebody wants too much from me or is trying to force me to do something I don't want to do.

I need to think through *what I really want* and how to respond to the person.

I don't have to oblige that person.

I can say no, offer to meet them halfway, or ignore them.

But I don't have to let someone affect me deeply.

Nor do I have to overreact in a way that's not in my best interest.

Today *I can decide what I want* and move on.

I'm Not Always the Best Judge

Sometimes when I think I'm having a bad day, it might just mean that I didn't practice something that I have already learned to do or I need to practice it in a different way.

It may also mean that I'm just not paying enough attention to what I'm doing.

Sometimes when I think I'm having a good day, it might just be at somebody else's expense or I just haven't realized yet that I might be in trouble in some way.

LOL.

I'm not always the best judge of my good or bad days.

On Blaming Others

There are days when things aren't going right and I blame other people for it.

And it may be somebody else's fault.

But when I blame them, it only makes matters worse. People become defensive and angry.

It's best that I step back and let the dust settle a little to figure a good way to handle it.

It's always best to discuss it with the person. But instead of confronting them with blame, I could explain that I'm not comfortable with the situation. I can ask if there is some other way to resolve the situation. I can offer my own solution or a compromise. Or I can say respectfully that I really don't want to get involved.

Sometimes, it may be appropriate to not say or do anything at all—if possible.

But it's always best that I think things through and not make a knee-jerk decision.

Every Day I Invest in My Savings Account

Every time I have a good day, every day that I feel grateful and appreciate what I have, every day that I remember how good it all is—is a day that I have invested in myself.

It's like I have a savings account or an insurance policy helping me to counteract those days when I don't feel so good, when I don't feel like "it's all worth it," and when I feel like crawling into bed and not getting up.

On those days, I reach into my savings account and call upon those good memories.

That's my insurance policy against getting too far down or depressed.

They make me remember how good yesterday was.

It seems to be working out well this way, so I'm going to keep making deposits.

I really like remembering how good my life is and how much I'm enjoying it.

So, What's the Point?

I've come to realize that the point of all this is not so much to be happy—though I certainly don't want to be unhappy—that's pretty obvious.

I've come to realize that the point of all this is to keep myself involved. To get up out of bed and see what I can offer. To care about what's going on around me and do the best I can.

The truth is that things are going to happen no matter what.

But when I get involved and try to be helpful, I feel better.

For me, that's the point.

Don't Push the River, Let It Flow

There's an old saying: Don't push the river, let it flow.

I smile thinking of someone standing waist-deep in water trying to push it.

It's a silly image.

Yet, I tend to do that same thing.

I push things that really can't be pushed or that just move on their own.

And, silly me, I keep pushing them to go *where I want them to go*.

I do it way too often, and usually things don't go where I want them to go anyway.

The people around me start resenting me, and I end up feeling alienated and disappointed.

When I don't push so hard or don't push at all, things often turn out better than I wanted or expected.

Best of all, all of us, myself included, tend to be a lot less stressed.

So, today, I'll try not to push that river.

No Rules for Living

Have you noticed that there are no rules for living?

I have, and it's upsetting. I really want to know the rules and play the game the right way.

But for me that means I want to play it and I want to win it.

So, if there were rules, I would probably try to beat them, change them, work around them, or ignore them.

Actually, life does have rules. And that's why I'm in trouble a lot.

Because I'm always trying to beat them, change them, work around them, or ignore them.

And that's why I'm regularly making myself unhappy.

More No Rules for Living

There really are no rules for living. No requirements for membership. No instruction manual.

But there are pressures. And I've had to learn to deal with them.

The biggest pressures are often the ones I put on myself

Traffic jams make me impatient and irritable.

My boss wants something right away and I get resentful.

My significant other, children, siblings, parents, friends, creditors, the president—the list can go on—all are making demands.

Who's really putting the most pressure on me?

I'm learning that it's me.

What if I just step back for a moment?

Relax, like a duck letting water roll off its back?

Do I really have to rise to every challenge and/or do it immediately?

Who made those rules?

The only requirement I think I have is to enjoy my life and do the best I can.

About Showering

Some days I don't want to read these little encouragements.

I don't want to take the time to reflect or meditate.

I don't feel like thinking about the day ahead and how to deal with it.

I don't care about what I want to achieve today realistically.

I'm too tired. I'm late. I'm not in the mood. These messages are getting boring.

I get it.

Then I think of the person who once said to me, "Would you skip taking a shower?"

And the answer to that is, "Probably not."

And then I think, Okay, okay. I'll make the time.

There Is a Presence

I am learning that there is a presence or a spirit, a gift, that seems to exist around me.

Whatever it is named, whether it is God or Buddha or some force, I try to feel it.

I sit up. I close my eyes. And I try to breathe it in. I try to sense it not only in me but all around me.

Even though I cannot see this essence, this thing, I try to feel its presence as much as possible throughout the day.

It seems to comfort me, and gives me some serenity and strength that I need at times.

If nothing else, I consider it just a few moments of "time out." A little break. Rest time.

Aside from helping me to relax, it helps me feel again like I'm part of what's going on rather than fighting everything.

That really helps me.

I'm Not Missing My Old Ways of Coping

Since I've started spending time each day reinforcing positive thoughts and practicing new ways of dealing with life, I realize how much I'm not missing my old ways of coping.

I'm not missing arguing with people, feeling disappointed, frustrated, or alienated.

I'm not missing obsessing about things like I used to. I don't want to anymore.

There are too many things that I am enjoying today.

I'm enjoying the people around me.

I am accepting them more readily and feeling more relaxed with the situations that I find myself in.

Things are turning out okay, because I'm not imposing myself on every little thing.

I'm trying to participate like everyone else does.

As I practice appreciating people around me and enjoying things as they are, life has gotten easier, even better.

Comfortable, Not Perfect

I spend time each day reflecting on what I'm doing and how I'm feeling.

I used to think I was so smart, but I realize now that I'm just another person trying to do the best I can.

I am not perfect.

I used to put so much pressure on myself to be perfect.

I couldn't tolerate my making a mistake.

Now, it's only a matter of feeling comfortable with what I'm doing.

Daily reflection helps me with that.

I am learning that if I make a mistake, it doesn't mean that I'm not "good enough" or that I'm "less than" anyone else.

I am learning to be reasonable in how I perceive myself and my decisions.

Life isn't perfect, I will never be perfect, but I can feel comfortable with what I do and how I'm managing.

No More Headbanging

I try not to do life alone anymore.

When I do, I usually end up in conflict with everyone and everything.

A "head-on" approach usually ends up with me banging my head against a wall and giving myself a headache.

When I take time to think things through and ask for help, the headbanging stops.

I step back. Relax. I wait for some alternatives to come to mind.

It may not happen right away. I may have to wait, and that can be difficult.

I've also learned to talk with other people about whatever is going on and ask them for their ideas.

I think through the ideas that I'm comfortable with and try to use them.

Mostly, I've learned that temper tantrums cause more problems than they're worth.

Notes for Change

I have found it helpful to write little notes of encouragement for myself reminding me of the changes I've made or want to make.

In fact, I've even ripped pages out of a book like this one to help remind me.

I don't change by reading something once. I have to practice it over and over again.

Writing and reading little reminders help me to remember to practice.

I've placed sticky notes or scotch taped pages on my bathroom mirror, the refrigerator, in my car, on my desk at work, and on the phone.

I've written things like: just breathe, you're doing fine, think things through, today I will just listen, and so on.

These notes are valuable reminders.

Reminding me to change by practicing these changes.

Changing My Daily Habits to Change My Life

Changing is not easy. I resist. I get lazy. I get resentful. I think, why do I have to change?

But then I think about how I used to handle difficulties and how bad my old ways made me feel.

Okay, I think to myself, *just keep trying*.

Someone suggested some exercises that I could do to help myself become more open to change.

For example, it was suggested I drive different routes to work each day for a week.

Or that I change my radio station to something new. Perhaps to something I think I might not like. Maybe classical music. Do it for a week.

If I was left-handed, drive with my right—or drive with both hands on the wheel.

These exercises helped loosen me up a little bit to the idea that I could make changes.

How to Change My Daily Habits Even More

Here are more suggested changes to my daily habits that I could practice for a week:

- Comb my hair with a different hand (not easy),
- Change my hairstyle (very easy when you comb it with a different hand),
- Sit in a different chair each day when I watch TV,
- Watch a different show each day that I wouldn't normally watch,
- Eat foods I've never tried before.

At first, I thought this was silly, but then I realized how resistant I am to change.

It made me really look at myself and question my willingness to change.

If I wouldn't practice combing my hair with my weak hand, how could I expect to handle more difficult changes, like confronting my anger or fear?

I began to practice these daily suggestions—sometimes grudgingly. Silly, huh?

Duck Noises and Their Significance to Change

So, I've come to understand that changing is not as easy as it sounds.

I've also come to appreciate the benefits as well as the work that people have to do to change.

But I also realize that some change can actually be fun, if I lighten up a little.

It's not always drudgery, and I don't always have to beat myself up about it.

Want to laugh?

See what happens when you try feeding yourself with your non-dominant hand.

That'll make anyone lighten up.

Along these same lines, someone suggested that I might put my right hand under my left armpit and make duck noises (Quack. Quack.) when I start to take myself too seriously.

Today, when things get too difficult or I'm taking myself too seriously, I think about feeding myself with my nondominant hand or I start making duck noises.

What I'm Discovering About Change

I'm appreciating how important it is to change my daily activities as a way of becoming comfortable with changing the more difficult aspects of my life.

As I change my daily routines, my perceptions about change are changing too.

I'm not seeing change as being as overwhelming as I once did.

In fact, it's been kind of fun in a way.

It's making me think about how I used to do things and how I'm doing them now.

I'm paying more attention to what I'm doing now.

I realize that I don't have to be "stuck in my old ways," especially if they are not in my best interest.

Trying out new things has lifted my spirit and has helped me to see that I can cope with and make positive changes.

What a nice feeling—and a nice change!

I Think I'll Continue

As I try out changes in my daily routine and as I read more of these encouragements, I'm beginning to see that I really care about what's going on in my life.

I'm no longer as disappointed in myself or with the people around me. I'm much less bitter and depressed, or angry and withdrawn.

I'm beginning to like my new ways of acting and the changes I'm feeling as a result.

I like taking a few minutes every day reading these encouragements, thinking about how I can do things differently, how I can act or react differently, and recognizing how these positive changes are slowly happening in my life.

I think I'll continue.

When Someone or Something Is Disturbing Me

Lately, when I find that someone or something that someone did is disturbing me, I try to remember that he or she is just the same as me.

We are all trying to do the best we can.

I may not like it, but it doesn't mean that I have to do anything about it.

And I certainly don't have to say anything negative.

More and more I'm seeing and accepting things as they are, and not letting them affect me like they used to.

That's quite a change.

In fact, an even greater change is realizing how much happier I've become as a result—and how grateful I've become.

How grateful I am to see things as they are, recognize how I feel about them, and not have to do anything at all in response.

Wow.

Can I Be Generous Today?

By generous, I mean, can I truly give something away? Without wanting something in return?

Not just something material or monetary, but help and support?

Can I compliment someone today? Tell them what a good job they're doing?

Can I help someone even if I don't agree with or like that person?

Can I offer to pitch in and do something for them?

Or do I worry that it might take away something from me?

That I will lose something? Self-respect?

That it might bother me if someone sees me helping someone who I thought shouldn't be helped?

Does my pride get in the way? Do I worry that I'll feel foolish later?

The truth is: I lose nothing when I try to be nice.

It's just nice to be nice.

So, what'll it be today—can I be generous?

Acceptance as a Form of Cooperating

I'm beginning to understand that acceptance is a form of cooperating.

It doesn't mean I have to like something, agree with it, or agree to it.

But I need to cooperate with it.

I have to find a way to somehow "make do" with what's going on.

At least for the moment.

I can figure out other ways to deal with it later after I've had a chance to think it through.

When something happens that I don't like, it doesn't require me to get bent out of shape, or, sadly, to get somebody else bent out of shape either.

Today I ask myself when something happens that I don't like: Am I going to cooperate or am I going to war?

I think I'll cooperate.

When the Fog Lifts

It's funny how my mind works.

It's overcast and foggy outside today.

I can't see the skyline that I usually see outside my window.

It gets me a little confused and a little down, not being able to see what's usually there.

I realize that I also have days like that.

Days when I can't see in front of me.

Days when I don't see what I usually can see.

Days when events, my emotions, or other people's actions cloud my vision.

On those days, I've learned to take a deep breath and wait it out, knowing that not only will the fog lift, but also trusting that the usual skyline is still there, though I can't see it at the moment.

I seem to be developing a little faith that things will work out, even when I don't see very well.

Before I Can Forgive Someone Else

Before I can forgive someone for hurting me in some way, I have to think about what it was that I wanted so badly from them and didn't get.

Sometimes it amounts to my being self-centered—wanting things and wanting them my own way.

My having a temper tantrum of sorts.

When that happens, I need to stop holding my breath and change my perspective.

Stop getting upset over what I think I want and what I think I'm not getting.

Which isn't the fault of anyone else other than my making unreasonable demands.

So, lighten up, I say to myself.

Someone didn't hurt me.

Maybe I hurt them because of the way I was acting.

Maybe it's me who needs to apologize and ask for forgiveness.

I Have to Try Getting Honest

I have to try getting honest.

At least with myself.

I have to recognize and acknowledge how I feel.

At least to myself.

I hate having secrets.

They keep me feeling distant from everyone, especially the people I care about.

And the more I keep things secret, the more lonely and alienated I feel.

I get so upset looking at someone and thinking, *if you only knew* . . .

And how fearful I get thinking that you might find out.

I push my feelings so far down that sometimes I'm not even sure what the truth is anymore.

I really want to admit the truth, at least, to myself—and try at some point try to be honest with the people I'm closest to.

I hurt—and I don't want to keep hiding like this.

More About Trying to Be Honest

When I've tried to tell someone about how I'm feeling, I've gotten all balled up inside.

I've been afraid of being laughed at, feeling rejected, or belittled.

I've lost my temper at times or belittled someone back in response.

I might have stopped talking to that person, rejecting them like I felt rejected.

Today I see things differently

Sometimes people laugh when they hear something because it makes them nervous. It isn't necessarily a rejection. I just took it that way.

And someone who may have belittled me may have done so because they were treated that way themselves.

Today, I accept how I feel and understand that if someone reacts unsupportively, I don't have to react similarly.

I can let them know that I don't appreciate what they're saying or how they are acting.

I've become much more comfortable opening up to people.

About Being Too Hard on Myself

Sometimes I get down on myself. I don't think I'm doing good enough. I worry you think so too.

That's when I need to step back and ask, "Why am I being so hard on myself?

Ha.

Only yesterday I thought I was doing better than everyone and now, today, I'm worrying I'm not good enough.

I need a little realistic assessment here.

I'm just one more person trying to do the best I can. No better and no worse than anyone else.

No one is perfect.

And no one gets "kicked out" for making a mistake or for failing at times.

It's when I don't try, blame others, or belittle myself that I get into trouble.

Today, I do the best I can.

I learn from my mistakes, and I do some pretty good work along the way—and I acknowledge that others do too.

Now that's reality!

Learning to Take it Easy

Why Don't I Just Relax?

It seems that so much of the time I am in some sort of disagreement or conflict, either within myself or with someone else.

It's getting very tiresome.

I don't understand why I keep myself in constant turmoil.

Who am I really fighting with and why?

Seems to me that I need to stop arguing so much.

I need to say, "I've had enough! I want to quit making everything into a battle and have some peace in my life."

When I think those words and actually say them aloud to myself, it's so freeing.

My shoulders relax. My entire body eases up.

I'm finding it so nice to not make everything into a struggle.

To simply say, "Okay world, I'm done. It's not all that important."

Wow. How good that feels!

My Two Shoulders

One of my shoulders has a gray cloud on it, consisting of dark thoughts which trouble me.

They tell me not to trust myself or anyone else, filling me with insecurities and doubt.

My other shoulder has the beginning of a new and clear day, one I might be able to enjoy.

But it's not yet as large or as powerful as that dark cloud.

So, I keep filling the "clear day" shoulder with realistic thoughts and encouragements.

As simple as: what a great day this is, how grateful I am for everything I have, for what I'm accomplishing, and for what I might do today to make life better.

As I remind myself of these things, that dark cloud has gotten smaller, less powerful, and is affecting me much less.

I like that bright side shoulder and how large it's becoming, crowding out that dark side.

Easing Up on Pressure

In the past I've taken on too much, putting too much pressure on myself.

I still tend to do it.

I get overly involved with too many tasks at one time and get emotionally drained.

Anxiety sets in as I try to figure out how to get myself out from under my commitments.

And then I can get depressed, even immobilized.

I'm aware of this now and I don't want to continue doing it.

I now know not to take on too much. And if I start to, I cut back as quickly as possible.

Cutting back is okay today, and stopping completely is okay too.

I'm more comfortable now with saying, I'm sorry but I've over-committed myself.

People tend to be understanding, and I can always start again in a limited way, when it's appropriate and when I'm ready.

For Good Use

I once heard someone say that putting what you have to *good* use is more important than what you have *to use*.

So, now I ask myself, "Am I putting what I have to good use today?"

I don't concern myself with being happy with what I have, although I am very grateful.

Instead, I spend a little time each morning thinking about what I have that I can put to good use *for* someone or for some situation.

Something that will make things better or help things along a little.

That's a pretty good way to start the day.

So, what things do I have that I can put to good use today?

It's Getting Easier

I'm finding it so good to have a daily discipline of reading encouragements and reflecting on the day ahead.

My morning routine is especially helping me to be more patient and understanding.

I'm building a foundation in my life that I can rely on.

And I'm realizing that when things go wrong, I don't need to blame myself or someone else.

More and more I find myself taking the "high road" and using the tools and encouragements I've read.

I like reminding myself to be grateful, trying to take breaks during the day, and trying to be honest with myself about how I feel.

I'm even talking things over with other people more often, without being overbearing or overly fearful.

It's not always easy, but it's feeling good—and it's getting easier.

What's Becoming Really Important to Me

More important than the pressures of my job, than money worries, than the irritating traffic I deal with every day.

More important than that irksome coworker or that news headline that I disagreed with.

More important than that difference of opinion I had with my significant other, child, parent, or friend, is:

- my remembering how good life really is,
- my remembering that caring spirit that is growing within me,
- my remembering that it's a new day with new opportunities,
- my remembering how grateful I am for having all these people and things in my life,
- and my remembering how I might be of use, cooperating, helping, and relaxing with all these people and things.

How's that for perspective?

I think I might be better able to face today after remembering that.

Holding on to What Really Matters

Life changes. Things come and go.

Day-to-day situations differ: at work, at home, with friends and family, with plans.

Even the weather.

But I'm finding that changes bother me less and less as I hold on to what's more positive and powerful.

Instead of focusing on my being disappointed and irritable, I focus on what's important to me.

What I like and what I can do.

I think about these encouragements, what I've reflected upon, how good life is and what I have to offer to the day, rather than what the day should be offering me.

I'm beginning to think of this as being spiritual.

I never thought of it that way before.

The world around me may change, even quickly, but I'm finding myself calmer about it.

It's getting easier for me to cope with changes.

Making the Time

I try hard not to skip a day of reading these daily encouragements and reflecting.

I'm really enjoying these few moments each day in quiet meditation.

Spending time like this is like exercising, helping to stay strong emotionally and in balance.

The same way that exercise keeps me toned and in shape.

So, I ask myself: Did I take time this morning to exercise myself with encouragements and reflection?

Am I remembering that I can stop anytime and take a moment to reflect? The same way I can take a little time to do some exercise?

Do I remember to relax and enjoy this day? Just like how a little exercise, like a walk, might relax me and clear my mind.

I keep reminding myself that it's never too late to stop, take a break and reflect.

Exercise and Spiritual Development

Someone suggested that I add a little exercise into my daily routine.

Supposedly it gets the body's endorphins going, contributing to a feeling of well-being.

It would also make me feel better about myself physically, increasing my stamina.

But I thought: I don't have the time, I hate exercise, I'm too tired, and I have too much to do.

I was told, though, that it was really about perspective, the same way that I was handling my life with self-defeating excuses.

It was suggested that I not make it drudgery or too long.

Find an exercise I liked and start out doing only ten minutes.

I was told anybody can do ten minutes.

In fact, it was suggested that I set a timer, so I don't go past my ten minutes.

Ha. That made me want to do twelve, just to prove I could do more than ten.

How I Began Exercising Spiritually

I thought about what I might enjoy doing and the time of day that would be most conducive.

I thought I wouldn't mind taking a walk around the block before or after dinner.

I could listen to music. Or, I could reflect on something as I walked, like, "I'm feeling better and better about my life and what I'm doing."

I could also focus on my breathing, taking deep breaths—so it would be more like a walking meditation which I might enjoy.

A friend of mine told me she liked to dance to her favorite music for ten minutes.

I thought about plugging in my treadmill or pulling out my old weights.

I laughed thinking, Okay, I could get those things ready, but it didn't mean I have to use them.

That's my self-defeating humor.

Then I thought, just start walking. Take the first step.

Watch out for the Good Times

Ha. It's funny how when life starts going well, I have a tendency to slack off on things.

It's like I start to believe that everything is going so well because I'm managing it all by myself.

I don't need any help. I don't need reflection or encouragement. I don't need to exercise. I don't need a daily discipline.

Pretty soon, things start going downhill.

I forget that my life became better because I depended on daily reflection to keep me balanced and to help me sort through my reactions to what was happening in my life

When I forget that and think that I don't need a discipline, I start to slip backward, picking up many of my old habits.

Do I really want to go back there?

Trust and Faith

I really want everything to work out. But that usually means the way I want it to work out.

And when it doesn't, I can still get disappointed. Even disillusioned.

I know today that I have to let things go. Particularly my emotions.

Not getting what I want may cause me pain. But if I'm honest about it, I'm just being self-centered. Even childish.

I want what I want when I want it.

But we don't always get what we want, do we?

Besides, is what I want necessarily a good thing?

Maybe what's happened is equally as good or better—or the best that could have happened?

Can I accept a different outcome than what I hoped for?

Lately, I'm more able to keep an open mind about things.

I'm beginning to have trust and faith in the process.

Weathering Stress

There are still times when my life is so stressful, whether because of external factors or stresses that I've created in my own mind, unreasonable demands that I've placed on myself, that the best I can do is simply "hang in there."

That's okay. Rough periods happen and we weather them.

But I cannot forgo what I've learned to depend on which keeps me afloat.

I continue to reflect and meditate, read encouragements, and remind myself to be grateful.

I think about that old saying, "This too shall pass."

I use all the tools that I've learned.

And I remember all the other rough times I've been through and remind myself that I've gotten through them too.

Today, I may feel insecure or overwhelmed, but I know deep within me that I will be able to weather this and my life will return to normal.

That Damn Serenity Tool

I've learned many tools to help calm me down and think more clearly.

One tool that has helped me many times is known as The Serenity Prayer.

I was told that even if I did not believe in God that just reciting the words without using the word God would still be helpful.

So, I would repeat the following words over and over again until the panic passed and I settled down:

> Grant me the serenity to accept things I cannot change,
> courage to change the things I can,
> and the wisdom to know the difference

Some days, though, the best I could do was to grit my teeth and just repeat a shorter version

> Grant me the damn serenity.
> Grant me the damn serenity.
> Grant me the damn serenity.

Even that little bit helped to clear a pathway.

A Quick Minute

When I meditate and reflect, when I encourage myself and others, when I breathe in and seek the help and goodness of life, nurturing myself and my spirit, everything becomes calm and good.

I try to practice this consistently—not just when I am already upset.

I have little notes to myself reminding me to stop and take a break.

I don't have to do it for long periods of time. Just a quick minute is often good enough to replenish myself.

I've learned that the more I do it, the calmer and more clear-headed I am.

It brings a little order to my life when I feel unsure, some peacefulness when I get uncomfortable, and some compassion when I'm feeling disagreeable.

The more I practice it, the more I find it really works.

And now I'm going to close my eyes for a quick minute and breathe.

Bye.

The Bicycle Analogy

I once read that living a balanced life is like riding a bike.

It's as much about what you don't do as what you do.

To keep your balance, you need to stay still on the bike.

Too much movement and you'll wobble, maybe fall.

Eyes need to look straight ahead for the most part, focused as much as possible on what's in front of you.

Too much glancing to the sides will throw you off balance.

Too much speed and you may lose control.

Too little and you'll again begin to wobble like a top.

Practice makes perfect.

Then with little effort, we begin to gracefully ride.

Do Something Good

I get more from my daily reflections and encouragements when I think about turning them into action.

And how I turn them into action is to think about how I can be useful to people.

Helping helps me to feel more grateful.

So, I help others when I can.

Whether it's simply holding a door open, letting another driver get in the lane in front of me, or offering change to somebody in the check-out line who is fumbling to find theirs, I try to do an act of kindness.

Better still, if I can, I do it anonymously.

And then I try not to tell someone what I did (not so easy with my big ego).

Whatever I do, it's really not a big deal.

But it does make the day go better and makes me feel grateful.

That's a big deal!

Buy Myself a Cup of Coffee?

Buy myself a nice cup of coffee on the way to work? *Sure.*

Pay a premium price? *Well, okay.*

How about lunch out? *Yeah, I got to get away from the job.*

What about splurging on dinner? *Yes, I need to reward myself for what I'm going through.*

Time to reflect and meditate? *Can't, I'm running late.*

Think about how grateful I am for all that I have? *I'd like to, but I've got to finish this.*

Take some time to think things through? *Wish I could, but then I won't be able to go out tonight.*

On balance, without balance in my life, how important are all these other things?

If I can spend all that extra money on me, why would I not spend some extra time on me as well?

Today I will balance out my life—and take care of my inner me too.

When It's Difficult to Accept

It's difficult to accept when things turn out differently than what I want, expect, or hope for.

Some outcomes can be very unfair, downright rotten, or distressing.

Even harmful.

They can cause much pain and confusion.

I could spend time wishing they never happened. But to what effect?

I can try to change the outcomes, if possible.

Moreover, I can try to change myself, adjust and move on.

I can comfort myself sometimes with the knowledge that things and situations often change over time.

Few things, if any, remain the same.

So, what happened today may not stay that way or have the result the next time.

Mostly though, I take comfort in the fact that I continue to do the best I can and remain as grateful as I can for what I have.

Running the Show

Some force runs the universe.

Something created it, keeps it moving, and guides its motion.

What is it?

I don't know.

But I know this: I am not that something.

Some days I think I'm running the show, but ...

Call it what you will—Spirit of the Universe, the Divine Principle, God or Buddha, a Higher Power, Allah or the Almighty—I reflect on the fact that this force, this "something," exists and I appreciate its wonder.

I am in awe of it, grateful for its existence and to be part of it.

And I realize that all my efforts to control things, to "run the show," pale in comparison to the real show that continues, and has continued, all around me, throughout time.

What a perspective that is.

You Already Know What You Know Already

You already know what you know already.

Sounds kind of silly to even say, but it's true.

So, before I have a conversation with someone, especially someone who I already know has different, and maybe even antagonistic, ideas from mine, I try to clear my mind of everything I already know.

Because I already know what I know already.

This could be an opportunity for me to learn something new, understand why this person thinks differently from me. It might change my views.

But I have to really concentrate on what that person is saying.

I have to be careful not to "Yes, but" them or allow myself to mentally argue with them as they speak.

Everything that I know and believe in will not be lost because I'm listening, and ...

I might just learn something.

The Center of the Universe

Is there a center of the universe?

Sometimes I think I'm the center of my universe.

But if it's me, we're all in trouble.

Obviously I'm not, although sometimes I feel that way.

When I'm upset, down, or needy, I am the center of my own universe. And I need to attend to myself, take care of myself, and try to remember that I might just need to put myself first— before I can be of use to anybody else.

But ultimately, I know there is a center of the universe, and it is not me.

I am responsible for me, but something great created all this and permeates it all.

It is that center that I try to align myself with each day when I reflect, meditate, and read these encouragements.

I keep practicing learning new and different ways to perceive and act.

Journal for Encouragement

Keeping a journal is a great tool.

When I write, I spend less time obsessing.

I write about things that I would not be comfortable talking about with someone else.

I keep it safe, where no one else can find it. No one can see it unless I share it with them.

What freedom that gives me!

As a result, I'm knowing myself better—understanding my motives and why I behave as I do.

It's especially helpful when I go back and reread what I wrote a few days or weeks before.

But I have to be totally honest when I'm writing.

It's another form of meditation as I allow my thoughts to flow freely onto the paper, not censoring or judging myself.

It's just me admitting who I am to myself.

Can I get honest with myself?

An Awakening of My Spirit

Over time, with disappointments and frustrations, my spirit, my inner self, has waned and has become more guarded.

As I've felt hurt, I've tended to withdraw or give up.

Daily reflection counters that.

Taking time, especially each morning, has rekindled my spirit.

I like the quiet time, reflecting and thinking about something greater than myself.

Reading daily encouragements has helped me to see new ways to react to life.

It's keeping me on a higher plane.

I'm more comfortable now participating in the events around me in a reasonable manner.

I'm caring again—about life and the people near to me.

My spirit is becoming reawakened.

It's being nurtured, growing and so much less guarded.

I Will Let Myself Be Taken Care of Today

As I start my day and look around, I appreciate the natural greatness of the world: the warm sun, the green trees, the skies which seem to go on forever.

How could all of this have come to be?

It certainly wasn't any of my doing.

Sometimes I hear that small voice inside of me whispering, "Be grateful that there is something so powerful as to create all this. And all you have to do is relax and enjoy it. I'll take care of things."

Will I let myself enjoy this today? Can I relax enough to appreciate it all?

Or, do I still have to hold on tightly, trying to force everything to be the way I want it to be?

I think I'll try to relax and enjoy, and let myself be taken care of today.

More Activities to Change Spiritually

Here is where the rubber meets the road if I really want to change spiritually.

I treat people, even those I may not like at all, with respect and kindness.

I do this even if someone responds to me negatively with something like, "What do you want from me?"

I try to respond with something simple, like, "I'm just trying to be nice."

I've been pleasantly surprised how, more often than not, the other person has responded back positively.

Maybe not at first, but usually over time.

There have been a few people who have continues to react negatively, but I try to maintain positive thoughts about them regardless.

The point is that I am trying to live my life differently.

It's not about them.

It's about practicing my actions and reactions differently, in a more mature and measured manner.

Ha. It's really all about me.

Minding My Own Business: A Reminder

A hard thing for me to do is to mind my own business.

It's difficult enough being nice, meditating when I don't feel like it, or being honest with myself.

But mind my own business?

That's really tough.

For example, I don't like where you parked, what you said, and I especially don't like how you're dressed.

Get rid of that tie, I hate it.

Minding *your* business is second nature for me.

But minding my own business? And not minding yours?

That's a challenge!

Because I am so darn critical.

And it's hard to keep my negative thoughts to myself and, instead, find common ground or nice things to say.

I'm trying though.

As I try, I'm getting along with others better and having a good time.

Saying Please and Thank You

Saying *please* and *thank you* has become very important to me.

It has given me a realistic perspective.

It stops me from being demanding and acting unappreciatively.

I start my day now by looking upwards and asking, *Please let this day be a good one.*

Then I say, *And thank you for this day.*

When I say *please*, I'm no longer demanding.

I feel human, humbled, and a little vulnerable too.

I'm not used to that.

I may not receive what I'm asking for.

I may have to accept what's being offered to me, which sometimes may take time, or I may be given nothing at all.

But saying *thank you* allows me to be gracious—and grateful.

It reminds me to appreciate what I'm given, even if what I was given was nothing.

Sometimes nothing can be just what I need at the moment.

On Getting Rightsized

Everything I'm doing is helping me to get rightsized, to fit in.

That's all I've really wanted all along.

As I stop trying to be in charge of everyone and everything, it's getting easier.

I'm tired of trying to make everything happen the way I want.

The opposite of this is true too.

I do not want to be, nor do I want to feel like I am, controlled by anyone either.

It's been hard enough expecting me to be perfect and berating myself when I wasn't.

I know now that I'm neither the best nor the worst.

I don't want, or need, to be so critical—of myself or you!

I'm just another person trying to do the best I can, as you are, and I can use some help to do it.

I'm getting that help as I practice these things every day.

Watching, Waiting, and Being Helpful

Today I practice watching what others do without judging them or trying to control the situation.

I watch and I wait. Hoping to learn something.

I try to be aware of my reactions and think about what's going on around me.

If I have questions or have something to say, I'll say it.

But I don't criticize or try to take over.

I'll move on if things don't seem to be working out well.

But I do I ask myself before I move on *if* there is something else I can do?

I try to get out of myself and certainly get out of my own way.

I'm learning that I'm not dependent on others or on situations to make me happy.

I've become comfortable now knowing that I can help myself and be of help to others in most situations.

Today's My Day to Enjoy

Nobody spends as much time as I do being critical of me.

Nobody thinks about me as much as I do either.

If they do, they spend a moment or two and that's it.

Then they go on with the rest of their day.

So, why do I spend so much time focusing on myself and making myself miserable?

Why do I keep on second-guessing myself and worrying?

Whatever it is, it's over.

Next time I'll do better. I'll do it differently.

I'll apologize if I was wrong.

Maybe they'll apologize.

Maybe whatever I think happened wasn't that important to begin with.

Maybe nobody cares. It's just me that's worrying.

So—why am I making myself crazy?

It's time for me to stop and think about what I'm going to do to enjoy the rest of today?

On Not Stumbling Through Life

I feel like I have been stumbling through so much of my life.

Unsure of what I was doing.

Wondering what the purpose was.

Feeling unanchored and uncertain.

Disappointed or unhappy.

Questioning how I got this way and why I felt like I did.

But now I spend time each morning, and throughout the day, reflecting on what's important to me: being grateful for what I have, trying to be loving and patient, caring, and trying to contribute to the world around me.

I am no longer being "all take and no give."

Today, I try hard not to stumble.

I have purpose and I am grateful.

Each Day Is Different

Each day I find myself developing in different ways.

Today I might concentrate on having a little bit more courage.

Yesterday I might have been thinking about becoming more understanding.

Tomorrow I may focus on being more patient.

Maybe the day after I'll try to be less angry, or more loving, or try to put exercise into my life, and so on.

Every day becomes an opportunity for me to grow and face new challenges.

Most of all, I'm getting to be more open to change and to developing in new ways.

Encouraging Others

As I continue being grateful for what I have, I spend a lot more time thinking about what I can do for somebody else.

Is there something I can do for my significant other?

Maybe something as simple as a compliment, a hug, bringing flowers, or making their favorite meal?

Can I spend more time listening to and playing with my kids?

What can I do for any of my family or friends?

Is there someone at work that I might be able to help?

Maybe I can talk with someone about how my life has changed and how it's getting better?

I can share with them the things that I'm doing that are making me happier.

Is there some way I can encourage someone else today?

This is a good day to practice contributing to life.

I feel better already just thinking about it.

Two Sides to Everything

Have you ever noticed that there are two sides to almost everything?

Day and night. Up and down. Front and back. Right and wrong.

Nothing seems to exist without the other. And each has its own purpose.

I've come to understand that when I become active, afterward I need to rest.

After I experience joy, I need a chance to replenish myself.

When I feel sad, later I need to reflect on what happened.

Nothing stays the same. And I keep moving from one side to the other.

But at least now I'm moving.

I'm no longer stuck in one place, holding on to the more negative aspects of something.

I've gained a lot more trust and I'm becoming much more flexible about things.

All these tools that I've been learning and practicing are really making my life a lot easier and better.

Comfort Zones

Do I know my limits?

Do I know what I'm willing to do and what I'm not willing to do?

Am I willing to try to grow and stretch my limits?

And am I learning when I need to stop?

Do I handle my limits in healthy ways?

Stopping well before I go beyond my limits. Not taking on way too much.

Do I sometimes still cross the line into other people's business?

Have I learned when to mind my own business?

Do I tend to hide sometimes, afraid to find out what my limits are?

Do I play it safe? Maybe too safe?

What are my comfort zones today?

What is right and good for me today?

And can my limits change as I change?

Putting My Life in Perspective

Sometimes when I want to put my life into perspective, when I want to feel truly grateful, when I want to know my place in life, I think about a power of the universe, some greater being, God if you will.

And I imagine that eternal spirit as having a voice.

A voice which says to me, "Where were you when all this was created? Did you make the mountains rise? The wind blow? The sun come up? The rivers flow?"

Then I imagine that same voice whispering to me, "And who are you to question all this? Or me?"

I quickly sink back into my chair, settling in and settling down.

Giving Me a Break

There are times when I just don't take the time to reflect and meditate.

Times when I feel a little rebellious or annoyed.

Times when I feel that all this stuff isn't working as quickly as I'd like.

Times when it seems to take up too much of my time.

It was suggested to me that when these times happen—and they do—to go easy on myself, relax and take a break.

Everything will be okay.

So, on occasion, when I need to, I take a break.

Pressuring myself never does me any good.

Soon enough, I come back.

I need to. I've come to know that daily reflection and encouragements make my life better.

Easier.

Today I might give myself a break, the same way I might give others a break too.

And when I'm ready, I come back.

Back to Basics

When I get crazy, overwhelmed, down, or just plain worried, I go back to basics.

And the basics are this:

- I take it one day at a time,
- sometimes, I take it one-half day at a time, and
- when it's really bad, I just take it five minutes at a time.

I do much better handling life in small parcels.

It's called "baby steps."

Small little steps that I can handle.

I take it easy and I try to relax.

Sometimes I try to focus on my breathing, saying to myself that "I am breathing in the good and exhaling out all of my anxiety."

Sometimes the best I can do is just continue to breathe.

It's an Inside Job

When I try to change people who are affecting me, it takes up a lot of time.

I try to influence them to do what I want or argue with them about their opinions.

I get myself upset with them—and get them upset with me.

What works best is to just focus on myself.

When I reflect on what I'd like to do, what I can do, and what I don't want to do, I am much more productive, and happier.

I spend less time being upset with people and more time enjoying doing what I can do, to the best of my ability, while not stepping on other people's toes.

I might want the world to change, or I might want to change the world (ha!), but it's best just to try to change myself.

I like the expression that "It's an inside job."

Try a Gratitude List

I keep a gratitude list.

It's a list of things that I am grateful for.

Large and small, whatever they are, in whatever order.

For example, I'm grateful:

> *to be alive, to have use of my senses, to be able to read these reflections and to change, to appreciate this "Divine Force" in the universe, to have a roof over my head, food on the table, a family, some employment, people I care about, the sunrise, my morning coffee, all things large and small.*

The list goes on.

But I have to write it down.

I tend to forget the good things I have in my life.

I save the list, and I add to it.

I read it whenever life gets hard, so I remember all the things that I do have.

Gratitude is a great tool and defense against life wearing me down.

A Tough Pill to Swallow

Today's encouragement may be a tough pill to swallow:

It's important to have a daily discipline.

Honestly, I've always hated the idea of discipline. My rebellious side would always rebel. Ha.

But when I practice this discipline, it provides consistency in my life and a foundation that I can rely on.

It's really just a daily routine—which is much more acceptable to me than calling it a discipline.

When things go wrong, it helps me to not complain or blame other people.

It helps me to take the high road, see the good in things and make the best adjustments I can to some difficult situations.

The tools that I'm practicing are working.

Some days it's a tough pill to swallow, but things are turning out so much better.

It's All Good for Me Today

There is an old saying that I have read, which has stayed with me throughout the years, which is:

> I'm grateful for all that has been given me,
> I'm grateful for all that has been taken from me,
> and I'm grateful for what has been left for me.

Someone else once said it another way quite simply:

> It's all good.

Is it "all good" for me today?

That's not to say that bad things won't happen, but I believe that I will have the strength to cope.

I will cry over my losses, howl when things hurt too much, and talk about it when I don't know what else to do.

But I won't have to run away, I won't have to take it out on you—or on myself—anymore.

And because of that, *it's all good*.

Tools, Tools, and More Tools

Life is Getting so Much Better—and Easier

Each day that I take the time to read encouragements, reflect and be grateful, life gets better and easier.

I'm enjoying myself so much more, and I'm having fewer and fewer periods of being upset or irritable.

When I do have them, they don't last as long and are much less intense.

The tools are working!

Tools such as:

> taking a break, breathing, thinking about what I'm grateful for, reminding myself that someone else is doing the best they can, focusing on something I'd really like to do, taking a walk, saying the serenity prayer, thinking about what I can do for somebody else, doing something for someone else.

My life is really getting so much easier, so much better and I'm so much more grateful.

Thank you.

Positive Repetition

Most of these encouragements say the same thing.

So, why do I have to keep reading them?

It's the repetition that's helping me.

Doing the same good things over and over again—until they become habit.

Until I do them naturally. Not thinking about them anymore.

From the time we were young, we learned things through repetition, trial and error, and practice.

From feeding ourselves to tying our shoes, learning to read, and continuing on to learning how to dance, date, and drive. It doesn't stop.

It's practice, practice, and more practice.

Pretty basic, but that's how we learn.

And it's how I'm still learning today.

So, I keep reading and practicing, reading and practicing, and it's all becoming second nature.

Negative Repetition

I'm practicing new ways to deal with life through positive repetition.

When I repeat my old ways, I see how I made my life more difficult.

It reinforces for me how much harder it was before. I don't want to go backward.

I used to think the people around me were stubborn and inflexible.

I was right and they were wrong.

But these thoughts and reactions only created more disappointments, more frustrations, and more feelings of alienation.

Today, I'm on an upward learning curve.

I look forward to being on the positive side of life, repeating reasonable and realistic practices, encouraging myself and others to do well.

I enjoy stepping back, relaxing, and *smelling the roses*.

I'm much more comfortable in my own skin now.

It's because I'm replacing my old negative practices with new positive ones.

It's All About Change, Isn't It?

I keep practicing these new things over and over and over again.

I have to admit it gets tiresome from time to time.

But it's the best way I know to change my thinking, my perceptions, my reactions and, ultimately, my actions.

Repetition is the means of keeping the change going.

If I don't practice, I will slip back into my old ways.

And those old ways were not in anyone's best interest. Certainly not my own.

They were self-defeating.

So, I remind myself that it takes time and repetition to do this.

To learn to think differently.

To learn to perceive realistically.

To learn to react and behave reasonably.

I don't want my old ways back.

It may be tedious to do these new things repetitively but it's these new things I'm practicing that are helping me change.

On Being Bullied

There are times I meet up with bullies.

I have trouble controlling my reactions to them.

Sometimes I don't even realize I'm being bullied.

I feel intimidated—hurt and fearful.

I want to lash back, but my thoughts become jumbled.

I have to work really hard at overcoming my emotions.

I remind myself that I'm not confused.

The truth is I don't like being treated that way. And that's okay.

But I get caught off guard and then I have trouble standing up for myself.

So, I practice saying, "Tone it down."

Then when I see them again, I can say that they need to "take it down a peg if they want my attention."

If they won't, I can excuse myself and move on to things that are more productive.

My time is too precious to waste on bullies.

My Alone Time Helps Me with People Time

Today it all seems very simple.

The time that I spend alone each morning reflecting helps me to better enjoy the rest of my day with everyone else.

It gives me a chance to clear my mind, think through any concerns that may be lingering, reflect on how I want to handle them, and consider what I'd like to accomplish today.

I remember how grateful I am, which puts me in a positive frame of mind.

I then see things in a constructive and reasonable light, ready to encourage myself as well as everyone else that I come in contact with.

It's my alone time that helps me with my people time.

On Not Staying Upset

If I let myself stay upset, I leave myself open to becoming even more upset.

That door swings wide open to hundreds of other upsetting thoughts.

I replay old memories and resentments.

The "should have's" start. I should have said this or done that.

The "I hate's" also begin. I hate them. I hate feeling this way.

Even the dreaded, "I hate myself" or "I hate my life."

I really have to fight back.

But fighting back means making quiet time to clear my head.

So, I focus on many things: breathing, the serenity prayer, asking for help, journaling, exercising, talking with others.

I use my tools over and over until I feel calmer.

No need to keep myself upset. There are too many things that I like to do now in life.

All the Good Stuff

I try to center myself, get my thoughts straight, early in the day.

I now take regular advantage of quiet time, especially when I have rough moments.

And I enjoy taking refuge in the comfort of people who care about me—family, friends, and acquaintances from social groups that I've become involved with.

I enjoy thinking about what I can contribute to the people I care about and to the world around me.

I've begun to give freely of myself without looking for anything in return.

I ask people what they think they need. I listen to their answers.

I thank them for sharing their thoughts with me and for playing a part with me in trying to make things better.

I'm beginning to heal and I like healing.

The "Walking Through an Emotion" Tool

A tool that works well for me is: "walking myself through an emotion."

For example, if I'm angry, I imagine telling the person how wrong they are, even how stupid they are, and imagine myself really blasting them.

Then I think about how I'd feel afterward: shame and remorse.

I imagine the other person's reaction.

How hurt they might feel or how angry they might get.

I imagine them retaliating—worrying about what they might do.

I play this out until the bitter end.

Until I realize how futile this is.

Then I reflect on what made me angry and imagine myself reacting differently.

Talking with the other person about what happened, trying to work it out.

That works a lot better than attacking them or refusing to talk to them, and harboring resentments.

When I walk through an emotion, I see more clearly and behave reasonably and productively.

On Friends, Family and Social Groups

I'm appreciating how good it is to have family, friends, and social groups back in my life.

I need the closeness, the relaxation, and the recognition.

I haven't always allowed myself this.

My moodiness and negativity made it difficult for everyone.

It's wonderful to enjoy them once again.

I am realizing now how important my significant other is to me.

As well as family and friends.

How tolerant they have been with me and how intolerant I have been with them.

Practicing daily reflection has made a vast difference.

I'm so grateful to have them, enjoying who they are and seeing how they manage their own lives.

I'm trusting them and depending on them.

It's only because I make time each day to stop, think things through, and recognize how truly valuable these relationships are to me.

So, Nothing's Perfect?

I don't practice these daily encouragements perfectly.

Ha.

If I did, I'd be perfect.

And I wouldn't need to continue to practice.

I'd get it right the first time. And life would be perfect.

Yeah, right!

Now that's funny.

It's nice to be able to laugh at myself when I think this way.

I used to take myself so seriously.

I expected too much and pressured myself to do everything perfectly.

Today I can laugh at myself and my imperfections.

I practice not taking myself or life too seriously.

I might want the day to go perfectly and for me to be perfect—but now I know that "that ain't going to happen."

And knowing that it isn't, might make it a perfect day.

Now that's funny.

Treat the Whole Day Spiritually

I really enjoy my mornings of spiritual encouragements, feeling grateful, and thinking about the day ahead.

It struck me that I could treat the whole day the same way.

Especially because as the day goes on, I can get a little bent out of shape.

So, before I start something new, I reflect now on what I'd like to accomplish.

I relax and think about how grateful I am to be doing whatever it is.

I take my time doing it, and if I'm working with someone, I try to enjoy cooperating with them.

When it's over, I think about how grateful I was to take part in it.

If I feel uncomfortable about something, I consider how I can address it later.

When I treat the whole day like my mornings, the day is a lot more pleasurable.

If I forget, I can just stop and start again.

Not Perfect, but Definitely Better

Each day, each time, I read encouragements and reflect, I'm making progress.

I'm not becoming perfect. I never will be.

In fact, I don't want to try to be perfect anymore. It's too hard and I fail too often.

What I'm trying to do today is to live comfortably in my own skin.

I try to do the best I can for myself and for the people I care about.

And when I fall short, I reflect on my perceptions and how I could have reacted differently.

I've learned that it's not too hard to say *I'm sorry* or that *I was wrong*.

I'm learning to ask what I can do to set things right or to make up for it.

By my doing this, life is getting easier.

I'm handling my relationships more comfortably.

Is everything perfect? Definitely not!

But I'm grateful for the way it's become.

Self-honesty

A thorny issue I grapple with is being honest with myself.

While there are things I can't admit to you, there are some I don't even care to admit to myself.

I flinch just remembering them.

When I feel this way, I know I have to set things right.

I don't have to rush out and admit them to you, but I do have to start by getting honest about them with myself.

My usual reaction is to push them from my mind or deny them in some way.

But I have to admit that yes, I did this or yes, I said that.

Some of these things embarrass me to the point that I wish they had never happened.

But they did.

So, getting honest with myself is the first step, though not the only step, to my feeling whole again and having some inner peace.

Self-honesty Continued

Journaling is no easy task

I keep my notes private and safe. I'd be uncomfortable if someone read them.

Some things seem so disagreeable that I actually write them down differently than how they happened.

I've had to stop myself when I begin altering or softening them in some way.

I realize it's because I'm embarrassed—certainly not proud of myself.

It's difficult to face my thoughts, feelings, and actions.

But I don't want secrets anymore.

I don't want to lie about things, especially to myself.

I see myself repeating some of these behaviors even today.

I believe it's because I haven't fully faced them in my past.

If I do, then maybe I can handle them better today.

I don't want to keep repeating the same mistakes.

Today, I want to live differently, comfortably.

More Self-honesty

As I become more honest with myself, I'm more honest with others.

It was fear that was stopping me.

Fear of admitting that I didn't like my own actions and fear that you wouldn't like me in response.

I was embarrassed and ashamed of some of the things I did.

I couldn't concede that I was wrong or how guilty I felt.

By refusing to honestly acknowledge them, I could continue to think of myself as a "nice person."

Continue to believe you thought of me that way too.

Today, I can no longer keep these things secret.

I've become comfortable now recognizing and admitting when I'm wrong.

I can say *I'm sorry*, forgive myself and correct the situation.

Life isn't perfect. But fear and secrets no longer control me.

I've read that "The truth shall set you free."

I like being free. No more secrets.

What Happens After Self-honesty?

After acknowledging my wrongs, I have to set things right.

I owe an apology at the very least. More so, I need to undo whatever damage I did.

I think hard about what I can do.

I make sure I'm ready to hear what the person might say to me or ask of me.

I reflect deeply on whether what I'm about to do will be helpful.

If not, I don't do it.

I consider other things I might do instead.

I can write to people.

I can volunteer my time or donate to a charity as a means of paying back.

I can help someone else or do something in a way that will help make up for whatever damage I did previously.

But I need to take some action.

And I need to make sure I don't repeat these mistakes again.

Self-honesty, Not Other-honesty

When a disturbing situation happens, I look for my part in it.

Sometimes I point a finger at the other person.

I think, if he or she hadn't said or done this or that, I wouldn't have said or done what I did.

That may be true, but it doesn't excuse my behavior.

And if I accuse someone else, it only makes things worse.

I can only focus on me and what I did to make things worse.

The old saying comes to mind: Two wrongs don't make a right.

When I act poorly, I need to straighten it out. And do it quickly.

It's the only way I can live comfortably with myself.

It's up to somebody else to admit their faults—not for me to decide that for them.

It's enough today to just admit my own and set things right.

I don't need to blame anyone else.

Taking My Time

In my rush to get things done quickly, I often get involved in something too soon or too much.

I'm realizing how important it is, as well as how difficult it can be, to find the right moment to involve myself in something.

There have been times when the opposite happens. When I prefer not to get involved at all. My fears keep me at the edges of things. Even close to the door, so I can make that quick escape (ha).

But neither running away nor rushing in usually works well.

It's best when I take my time, watching what's going on, listening, and learning.

Then when I feel I have something to offer, I can join in.

Sometimes the opportunity even presents itself to me.

Rather than rushing or avoiding, if I take my time the right moment seems to come.

What Are My Ideals?

My ideals today are not lofty or unachievable goals, but behaviors that I can practice, such as:

- no longer lying to myself or harboring secrets,
- attempting to live with the least amount of fear possible,
- behaving in a caring and patient manner,
- forgiving myself and others,
- finding joy in life and being grateful for what I have,
- loving and accepting being loved,
- working productively and cooperating with others,
- and being creative, giving, and hopeful.

Nothing is perfect. But, at least today, I have behaviors that align with goals that are reasonable and realistic to achieve.

I certainly haven't had, or believed in, enough of them in the past.

To the degree that I now practice them, I am so much happier and more involved.

Round Pegs into Square Holes

I still find myself, as that old saying goes, trying to put "round pegs into square holes."

I continue to make myself unhappy because, darn it, no matter how hard I try, I can't get those pegs to cooperate and those holes to accept what I want to put in them.

So, I chip away at the pegs and scrape out the holes.

After a while, nothing looks right, feels right, and everything is either notched or misshapen.

When will I learn to leave things be?

Leave the pegs and the holes just as they are.

They each belong in their own place—where they fit

When will I learn to allow myself to find the best place that I fit in?

Usually, that place is right where I am right now.

I'm fine just as I am and where I am, at least for today.

My Own Security Blanket

Some days I really need to be comforted. I feel shaky and insecure.

I know that you can't do that for me. When I get this way, nobody can.

I've learned though to give myself the reassurance that I need.

I imagine putting my arms around my own shoulders. Sometimes I'll even wrap a comfortable blanket around me.

I remind myself that I'm okay, and to stop stoking my own fears and anxieties.

I focus on my breathing and think about all the things I'm grateful for.

I baby myself. I remind myself to be kind to myself.

I can be my own security blanket. At least for today.

The truth is I do this every day by encouraging myself, reflecting, and taking the actions to keep my life, as much as possible, in balance—reasonable and realistic.

And what great comfort it's giving me.

So, When Will I Be Happy?

Some days I am happy.

Other days, I wonder when I will be happy.

On those days I wonder what I'm going to have to face today? What new battles? New fights?

And why?

I'm coming to see the truth though: there are no new fights.

The only fight I'm having is the one within myself, and with myself.

That's the fight that, on those days, I have to overcome.

If I treat each day as an opportunity, to embrace new things, to understand, to care, and to take a positive part in them, then I can and will be happy that day.

I'll even have an opportunity to make the people around me happy too.

So, when will I be happy? Today can be the day.

A Demand vs. A Request

I want things. Doesn't everybody?

A new car. A nice house. Respect. Love. Peace of mind.

Nothing's wrong with that.

But when I don't get what I want, I tend to think that these things are being deliberately withheld from me.

I start demanding my "fair share." What I feel rightly belongs to me.

And then my troubles begin.

Life, and other people, don't often concede to demands.

But when I ask for something, even request it, I'm on solid ground.

I may or may not get it. But no matter what, I move on.

When I demand, I don't move on.

Everybody loses.

I tend to take prisoners and, ultimately, I become a prisoner of my own demands.

Today, I try not to take prisoners.

I try to ask for what I want and accept what comes back to me.

Life's a lot more peaceful that way.

The Opposite of Demanding

Sometimes I get apprehensive about asking for something because in the past I didn't ask, I demanded.

I thought I was asking, but I wasn't.

I'd browbeat you if you said *no*.

I'd respond with anger to the point of rejecting you.

So, today I get timid about asking.

I'm not always certain how to ask, comfortable about whether what I'm asking for is reasonable, and I'm still sensitive to a "no" response.

But I take my time now, considering how I'll ask and what it is I'm looking for.

If someone says *no* now, I'm not as concerned.

I understand that someone might not be able to, or might not want to, give me what I'm asking for.

I know now it's not personal.

Similarly, I realize I say *no* to people as well—and it's not personal.

Today I can just ask and accept the answer.

Not bad.

Where Am I Going with All This?

I find myself wondering sometimes, where am I going with all this?

What am I really accomplishing?

Some days I'm confident in answering that question.

Other days, I'm not.

On those days, it's unsettling to feel that way.

But I need to trust that if I'm trying my best, correcting my mistakes as I go along, helping myself and others, being forgiving, then I'm on the right track.

Ultimately, I don't need to know where it's all leading.

I only need to know that I'm heading in a good direction and accomplishing, at least, what I can for today.

Realistically, I can't ask for more than that, can I?

That seems pretty darn good as it is.

On Panic Attacks

I still have days when I panic.

My mind races to the future playing "mental tapes," morbidly imagining every terrible thing that could happen.

But it isn't realistic.

As I practice daily encouragements, I'm building new "mental tapes" that are positive and help lessen anxiety.

They remind me to take certain actions, so that I'm not fighting anxiety only in my head.

So, I get up and walk. Exercise. Read uplifting words. Breathe.

I repeat positive sentences that relax me.

I talk with someone I trust.

None of the terrible things I've imagined happen.

It's been me terrorizing myself mentally.

Today, I have a spiritual force in my life which "has my back."

And I'm learning that anxiety is my body's way of telling me to take action.

So, I reflect, come up with a reasonable plan, and get myself going.

Fear and Doubt—Kissin' Cuzins

I read that there are two sides to anxiety: fear and doubt.

Fear kept me thinking that the worst will happen.

I hadn't thought much about doubt.

I realize now how big an influence it has.

I doubted that whatever good I might do to correct my situation would work. Somebody or something would undo it. So, I wouldn't even try.

It was a double whammy: fear believing something bad will happen and doubt that I could stop it.

Today I know that's not true.

I can realistically look at a situation and decide to do some beginning steps. I don't believe anymore that whatever I do will be unacceptable or rejected.

When I think things through, doing a little at a time, I'm able to set things straight.

I don't expect specific answers. I just look for good things to happen.

They usually work out.

Developing Spiritually

These daily encouragements are really putting me on a solid footing.

I have become so much more reasonable and realistic in my perceptions and actions.

It's given me courage and made me care about what I do.

I really can say today that I am growing in spirit, or, better yet, spiritually.

Each day as I reflect, I'm better able to see how I can participate and contribute positively to situations and to the people around me.

I'm beginning to think: is there anything more important than that?

I'm not living in fear and doubt like I used to. I have my moments. But they've become a lot less.

Today I'm accomplishing what I'm beginning to understand as the purpose of living. I am a part of what's going on and doing it in a good and healthy way.

I'm beginning to see that as true spiritual development.

Einstein's Constant

Einstein wrote that there is a constant in the universe. He wrote it as $E=MC^2$.

I've come to realize that I need a constant in my life.

Without it, I'm like a planet bouncing around haphazardly in the universe.

Loose, lost, and lonely.

Today I have that constant.

These daily encouragements along with the time I take to meditate and reflect, to feel grateful, to think about what I might offer in the day ahead, and how I want to be patient, caring, and forgiving— these are variables in the equation for me.

As I practice these things each day, I know my place in the universe.

I am exactly where I belong in the scheme of things.

I have what Einstein described: a constant.

A Mind Stretching Concept

Imagine allowing life to happen as it does.

What a difficult concept!

I had to bring it down to earth to understand it better.

For example, could I just watch what people did without judging them or wanting them to do things differently?

Could I watch situations evolve without interfering? Without jumping in immediately? Or, without worrying about them and avoiding them?

Could I look inside myself and ask what would make me happy—without denying somebody else's happiness?

Could I ask for something without demanding? And move on if it didn't work out?

Could I consider something else that might satisfy me instead?

Could I appreciate things just as they are? Not wishing they would be different.

Could I become less dependent on events and other people to make me happy?

Imagine if I could stop holding on so tightly and accept life as it happens.

Time Apart and Time to Be Part of

Today's encouragement is simple.

Sometimes I just need a simple encouragement.

The time that I spend alone each day, reading encouragements and reflecting, makes me more peaceful and comfortable with everybody else during the rest of the day.

It's funny how my time apart helps me to be better able to be part of everything else.

And for that, I am grateful.

Continuing with the Mind Stretching Concept

Slowly I'm able to sit back and watch events happen without injecting myself and my opinions into every situation—or avoiding them.

I participate but mostly by watching, listening, and learning.

That's working out much better.

Certainly preferable to when I used to insist I knew a better way and getting overly involved.

Or, preferable to those times when I'd get anxious about being asked to become involved, worrying that I might fail and backing away completely.

I am much less tense; the people around me are less tense too.

Some people have told me that I've changed.

They even offer now to help me. How nice!

I no longer hear, Who asked for your opinion? or Why do you always have to get in the middle of everything? Or, what makes you an expert?

I think I'll continue sitting back and watching.

We're all a lot happier.

Differences

I'm coming to understand, as I'm opening up with others about how I'm encouraging myself and changing, that each of us develops ourselves in different ways.

And most of us want some form of help to do it.

We may be working on something new on any given day.

Today, it may be about asking for courage.

Yesterday, it might have been about developing patience.

Tomorrow, you or I might focus on freeing ourselves from anger or fear.

We might concentrate on becoming more understanding or loving.

Other days, it could be about eating healthy or exercising to better our mental and physical well-being.

Or, we might reflect on what we have to offer to our community. How to volunteer our time.

There are so many things to consider and each of us approaches them differently.

How nice.

The High Road

I'm appreciating more and more what it means to take *The High Road*.

It takes patience, understanding, and trust.

It means that when things get rough, I won't blame somebody else or start to complain.

It means that I rely on the encouragements I read each day and practice doing.

It means stepping back, reflecting, breathing, being grateful, rejuvenating my spirit, and deciding on reasonable and realistic ways to handle myself and the situation I'm facing.

It's getting much easier to do.

But *The High Road* can still be a bumpy road.

That's to be expected, even after years of practice.

After all, nothing and no one is perfect.

We're all doing the best we can.

Tools for Settling Down

Many times I need to *quiet my mind*.

Thoughts race through my head; my brain is working overtime on something.

I have to use many tools to distract myself:

- I listen to music. Often without lyrics. Or, what's called *white noise*, like rain.
- Some people dance to music. Movement distracts from thinking.
- I'll sit and meditate, repeating a phrase either mentally or aloud like, *It's all good today.* Or I chant nonsense like, *Shushenpadmeladeeahhhhh.* Again, distracting me from thought. I take deep breaths, exhaling longer than my inhales.
- I go for walks, outside or just around the house. I exercise, write an email to a friend, or call a friend. I'll journal. Some people clean house. Some people pray.

I have to help myself to settle down; taking action quiets my mind.

Some days I have to work hard at it. Ha.

A New Perspective on Limits

I have limits.

I'm learning what they are.

I didn't always recognize them and that got me into trouble.

I realize now how much I need them.

I still stretch my limits from time to time, which can be good, yet it's important to know when to stay within my comfort zone.

There is, though, another side to this.

We live in a world that is limited to what we can see, hear, and feel.

In the morning when I reflect, I think about how much more there is than my limited vision.

For instance, how the universe goes on forever.

I am in awe of it.

Then, when I consider my problems alongside the vastness of space, I realize how insignificant they are.

It's then that I just want to feel in harmony with what I'm perceiving as this eternal entity.

That's pretty powerful.

My Savings Account

It was suggested that I consider the time I spend reflecting, encouraging myself, meditating, being grateful, and practicing new behaviors as being similar to making deposits into a savings account.

And not only are these deposits safe but they also pay dividends over time.

Most importantly, when things get rough, I have a wealth of spiritual and emotional reserves that I can withdraw to get me through.

I like that idea.

I do draw down some of my savings when the going gets rough.

And I'm grateful that I have saved up enough to help me get through those times.

I don't need to withdraw a lot or even often because of how much I am practicing living life differently.

I consider what I'm doing as a great investment and hedge against difficult times.

And I want to keep growing and investing in myself and my future.

Am I Continuing to Exercise?

One thing I can get complacent about is exercise.

It was suggested that I start with only ten minutes of exercise.

I was told anybody can do ten minutes—and the benefits are great.

But sometimes I get lazy. Sometimes I get too busy.

All excuses.

But I know that when I start back again, I feel so much better.

The truth is I like doing even more than ten minutes of exercise.

It really gets me going.

I find ways to keep myself interested.

I do different exercises on different days of the week.

I'll watch a movie while I'm on my treadmill.

I challenge myself to increase my weights a little or work out a little longer than usual.

I'll do some group sports or workouts.

I try to make it interesting, challenging and fun—so I don't get complacent.

Speed Limits and Spiritual Change

Speed limits.

Many people have issues with speed limits.

Some people always speed. Others are afraid of speed, driving well under the speed limit.

So, what does this have to do with spiritual development and change?

An exercise that I've tried while driving is to glance at my speedometer every few minutes and check my speed.

If I was speeding, I'd slow down. If I was slow, I'd speed up.

The goal became keeping myself close to the posted speed limit.

The point?

First of all, it's practice trying to stay at the same level, like being balanced, lessening the highs and lows.

It's also a way to manage my life, watching what I'm doing and adjusting as I need.

Today I try to be mindful not only of my speed but what I do.

I try to keep my life level, practicing spiritual speed and reasonable limits.

Back to Basics for the Moment

I've been practicing different physical activities and exercises to help me change.

As much as I want to change, I still need to focus on the basics.

I remind myself early in the day, preferably first thing in the morning, to read encouragements, meditate, reflect on the day ahead, and remember what I'm grateful for.

I still retreat into quiet times during the day to relax, especially if I'm getting irritable.

I'm spending more time with the people that I care about. My family, friends, and social groups.

And, as importantly, I think about what I have to offer.

I ask people what they might need.

I remind myself to listen and thank people for their feedback.

And, not so oddly, I feel like I might be helping to make the world a little bit better.

Minding My Own Business: A Reminder

It's still a hard thing for me to mind my own business.

It's difficult enough being nice, to reflect when I don't feel like it, or to be honest with myself.

But mind my own business? That's tough.

I don't like where you parked, what you said, and I especially don't like what you did.

Besides, I don't even like the way you're dressed.

Minding your business still comes naturally to me at times.

I can be so darn critical.

It's hard to keep my negative thoughts to myself, find common ground or have nice things to say.

I keep practicing though—listening without judging, trying to make small talk, and genuinely enjoying a conversation.

When I do that, I relax and I have a good time.

Trusting the Process

I want things to work out, but they don't always work out the way I want.

When this happens, obviously I'm disappointed.

But I work at moving on now.

I try to understand that *what I wanted* was just that—*what I wanted*.

And I'm seeing that many outcomes are better than what I wanted.

Maybe not initially or not for me, but over time I can see how good they can be.

Sometimes better for others, and that's good too.

If I practice slowing down, thinking things through, reflecting on what I wanted, and seeing what really happened, then I understand things better.

There's a process going on.

And I am learning to trust the process.

It doesn't always work out perfectly.

And often my idea of "perfectly" is getting what I want.

But the process does work.

Especially when I cooperate.

More Good Things to Come

If I am grateful—grateful for what I have up to this day—why would I not think more good things will come my way?

No matter if this day is frustrating, disappointing, or difficult, it will not be this way for long.

Everything changes.

But I will always have what I have received to this point and am grateful for today.

Some good things have gone from my life and I miss them, but not the gratitude I felt for having them.

And some things I still have and enjoy, and continue to be grateful for.

So, on balance, if it's been good to this point, why then would it not continue to be so?

Or even more so?

Today, and every day, that I am grateful—that feeling of gratitude will continue to fill me and will help carry me through any difficult times to come.

When I Eat My Spiritual Development

I've had to give some thought to how I eat.

For example, do I wait until I'm starving before I eat? Do I gobble down my food? Do I skip meals?

How about eating on the run?

Do I eat seconds and thirds? Overeat? Refuse to eat certain foods? Am I a picky eater?

Here's some more: Do I play with my food? Do I push my food around on my plate? Especially the food that I really don't want to eat.

Do I complain about my food? Too hot or too cold? Too spicy or not enough spice?

How I eat can be a lot like my spiritual life.

So now I'm taking time to observe my eating habits.

I'm beginning to think that it does reflect how I live and act.

More Eating My Spiritual Development

I'm seeing that how I eat reflects how I am spiritually.

As a result, I'm asking myself what I need to change.

If I'm eating too fast, I need to slow down.

If I'm skipping meals, I need to eat regularly.

If I'm eating on the go, I need to plan ahead.

If I'm eating unhealthy foods, I need to find ones that are healthier for me.

This is not any different than what I reflect upon when it comes to my own perceptions and behaviors.

For example, skipping meals is like skipping reading encouragements or reflecting.

Eating when I get to the point of starving is no different than having not sought answers until I'm already in an emotional jackpot, an immediate crisis of some sort.

I need to give thought to how I'm eating, the same as I give thought to living my life.

How I Eat and Spiritual Development

How I eat and how I live my life wouldn't seem to have much in common, yet I'm seeing so many parallels.

Do I slowly chew my food? Enjoy what I'm eating?

Can I identify the flavors? Do I ever close my eyes and savor how good the food tastes?

Do I take time in-between bites?

When I'm eating with company do I put my utensils down and listen? Or do I shovel food into my mouth in between sentences?

Do I eat slowly enough to realize when I'm full?

When I am full, do I stop? Or, do I continue on past my limits?

I've learned a lot observing how I eat and making the same efforts to moderate the way I'm eating as I do to moderate how I live.

Try paying attention to the way you're eating for the next few days.

See what you can learn.

Now That I'm Paying Attention

Just like I need to encourage myself and reflect daily, I need to maintain my efforts to concentrate on my eating habits.

I need to eat regularly and eat healthy foods.

I need to take my time when I eat and enjoy my meals.

I need to make conscious decisions about what, how, and when I eat.

I also need to keep up with daily exercise. All I really need is 10 minutes each day.

I need to remember that if I lapse back on exercise and my eating habits, then chances are I will lapse back on my daily reflections.

And if that happens, I will go back to how I was.

And I do not want to start behaving or perceiving like I used to.

Overcoming Adversity

Talking with Other People Who Struggle

Today, when I see people who seem to be struggling as I have, I make an effort to talk with them.

If they're open to it, I tell them what I was like, what I'm doing now and how it's working for me.

I listen to what they tell me they've been through, how they're coping, and what's working for them.

It's comforting to know I'm not alone and comforting to know that other people may feel comforted knowing they're not alone either.

Remembering what I've gone through and hearing what other people have gone through, reminds me to be grateful.

It keeps my memory fresh about how my life used to be, so I remember I don't want to go back to the way it was.

I like the way it is now. I want to keep it going.

Deep Down I'm Believing All Is Well

With all this daily reflection, reading of encouragements, and practicing living differently, I have come to realize that deep down within me all is well.

Life is going along as it should be, and I am happy and content with my life.

Certainly, there are ups and downs, bumps in the road along the way, but I am now believing that it's all good.

Everything works out.

Whether I try to change something, change me, change you, or just sit back and wait for change by going along for the ride, watching and waiting, it all seems to work out.

Deep inside of me, I'm feeling it's all pretty good.

My life doesn't have many wild swings anymore.

I like what's happened.

On Stability

Today I was reflecting on how stable my life has become.

And it's become stable because I have stopped demanding that things go my way—and conversely, I no longer refuse to ask for something for fear of being rejected.

I have learned to try to contribute to situations, offer my help, and participate rather than criticize or hold back.

I've learned to ask questions, to listen and learn, and ask what I can do to pitch in—rather than deciding for myself what needs to be done, believing I know best, and then just going ahead and doing it.

I've learned to wait and watch, seeing what opportunities may arise, and cooperating with people.

Today my life has become quite stable.

I'm grateful for it and I like it that way.

The Benefits of Verbal and Physical Activities

There are days when I do verbal or physical activities to relax.

I'll sit still and chant a mantra, a phrase that I can repeat easily like, *the world is as it should be and I am part of it all.*

Then I focus on my breathing. Exhaling longer than I inhale.

I might repeat the words aloud or just recite them mentally.

For physical activity, I walk. Either in my house or outside.

I do a similar thing as I walk, focusing on my breathing.

Exhaling longer than I inhale.

I can combine the verbal and the physical.

I can walk and chant. Aloud or mentally.

Some call this a walking meditation.

I do either for five minutes up to twenty minutes or more.

These activities help free me from obsessing.

The Lock on My Inner Peace

I've begun to have so much inner peace now and I tap into it almost daily.

I think of it as my job: My job maintaining my inner peace.

I try to keep out disturbing thoughts. I recognize them but I also recognize that I don't have to address them now. I work at not allowing them to dominate my thinking.

When it makes sense, I'll guard against these thoughts by reflecting on what can I do to ensure that they won't happen. Is there something I can do today?

Mostly I focus on how things are right now. And right now, everything's pretty good.

I go back to concentrating on my breathing, how grateful I am, and what I hope to accomplish today.

Then I put the lock on the door.

I have my inner peace and I try to keep it safe.

Win or Lose? It's My Choice

If I stop reflecting, if I become too busy, or other things are too important, I lose.

I lose perspective, balance, hope, and understanding

I gain irritation, disappointment, lack of perspective, and—ha!—even weight.

If I reflect each day, especially first thing in the morning, I win.

I win the respect of others, my self-respect, and the ability to consider what I have to contribute to the day.

I lose the bumps on my head from banging into walls, stumbling around blindly, and wasting my and other people's time.

Win or lose. It's my choice.

That's something for me to truly reflect on today.

Never Too Late to Change

It's never too late to change.

Sounds too simple. But it's true.

Yet how many of us actually try?

I know I've let many things slide by even though I knew they were good for me.

Some were insignificant, so passing them up was not so important.

But other things, *well, you know,* I avoided.

I said that I was too busy, there's too much going on, nobody will care (I hope) or know.

Sound familiar?

What stops me from making changes? From doing things that may be good for me?

Pride? Laziness? Fear?

The truth is that if something needs to be changed, I can change it.

And all the obstacles I put in the way are just that—obstacles I put in the way.

Maybe it's time to clear the way, get rid of the obstacles.

It's not too late.

My Fear of Action

Sometimes I have crippling fear *after* I take an action.

Other times I have crippling fear *just thinking* about an action that I might take.

I've learned that both of these fears are the same.

I call them *what-if's?*

What if they don't like it? *What if* I fail? *What if* I can't fix it? *What if* I get into trouble?

Then I have the *I'm-sure's, I'm-not's,* and the *I-am's.*

I'm sure it won't work. *I'm not* up to this. *I am* inadequate.

Then comes the futuristic predictions.

They'll know I'm a failure. *I'll be* humiliated.

These are only thoughts, though. Not realities.

But they still make me panicky.

Even reading about them can make me anxious.

Which makes me realize even more how all this is only in my mind.

Later, when I calm down, I might *rationally* decide to do something that's manageable for me.

More Fear of Action

When I'm overwhelmed at taking some action, I can refuse to "step out of the box."

I can withdraw completely.

Why am I like that?

I know I'm trying to protect myself from fears of failing.

People who care about me get frustrated. Even coworkers and friends get disappointed with me.

They believe I can do it and implore me to *just try*.

Embarrassed, I can just stare at them, overwhelmed by anxiety.

Today, I remind myself to breathe and use every tool available to me.

I've learned that I don't need to do anything right now. I just need to quiet myself down.

I remind myself that I can do that.

And once I've calmed down, I might consider something manageable that I can do just for today.

And then I do it, and begin feeling better.

All is not lost.

Overcoming Fear and Inaction

When I fear some new activity, I need a reality check.

Reality is that: I have rarely failed and certainly haven't failed completely.

Reality is that: when things have gone wrong, I've made adjustments.

Reality is that: new activities usually are not completed all at once. There is a process, usually undertaken in small manageable increments. Baby steps.

Reality is that: there are usually bumps in the road

Reality is that: most times it's a group effort.

So, I focus on these realities.

And I remember that only an unwise person will jump into an unknown body of water.

Most of us will dip our toes in the water. Acclimate ourselves to the temperature. Make sure it's safe to swim.

That's all I have to do today.

And remind myself that it doesn't all rest upon my shoulders.

And now the fear and pressure slip away.

A Few Constants That I Can Rely On. Ha!

There are a few constants that I can rely on.

First, everything changes.

If I rely on that, then I don't have to worry about tomorrow.

Another constant is being grateful.

I am grateful when everything is good, but can I just as easily be grateful when things aren't?

When things don't go my way, it can be just as well.

Some things cause more problems than they are worth.

So, it's possible I can be grateful when things don't work out.

Another constant is faith.

I have faith in the first two constants: everything changes and feeling grateful.

A final constant is: when I try to keep everything the same, I get into trouble.

Reading Encouragements Several Times A Day

I've gotten into a habit of reading these encouragements throughout the day.

I have them in my office, on my mirror in the bathroom, and even on the dashboard of my car.

I refer back to them often.

I need the repetition.

And I need to read them especially when I start to feel stressed or anxious.

They are great reminders helping me relax and feel comforted.

I like taking time to reflect and encourage myself throughout the day.

I need that feeling of security—of "me" time.

The repetition of reading encouragements also reminds me to practice what I'm learning.

When I'm Upset with You, I'm Really Upset with Myself

When I criticize you, it's me I'm talking about.

When I tell you that you're stubborn, it's me being stubborn by only wanting you to change your mind, not me to change mine.

When I tell you how angry you're making me, it's me making myself angry because I'm not getting my own way.

When I tell you that you're hurting me, it's me hurting myself because of my inflexible insistence on accepting only the answers I want to hear.

It's me being stubborn, angry, and hurting myself. Not you.

When I suggest *what I'd like* to see happen, rather than demand it, then, maybe, we can have a conversation.

And *when I can listen* to your concerns and consider them, then, maybe, we can work things out.

But it can only happen when I stop making one-sided demands and stop blaming you for not agreeing to them.

Shelter from the Storm

We all need a place to feel safe.

A refuge. Shelter from the storm.

I certainly do.

Sometimes it's a physical space.

A place where I can be alone and feel comfortable without worrying about somebody intruding or observing me.

But going there is not always possible, so I have to create another kind of shelter.

A safe place in my mind.

It's not always easy.

But I practice.

I might take a few moments, closing my eyes and focusing my attention elsewhere.

I might imagine being in my usual "safe physical space."

I might repeat a phrase that brings me comfort.

I might take a few deep breaths, breathing out any stress I'm feeling.

I take shelter from the storm when I need it and how I can get there.

I don't wait until I can be totally alone in that physical space.

The Watermelon Patch

Our neighbors had this great garden.

At the end of the season, several watermelons were left over and the neighbors had gone on vacation for a few weeks.

As we drove by, I wondered aloud to my wife that if we took one would they notice or even mind.

She told me that she had spoken with another neighbor who wondered the same thing.

They thought the chances were slim to none that it would be noticed.

But, after discussing it, they agreed that the guilty feelings that would follow after taking one, without their permission, would probably ensure that when they ate a slice, it would leave a sour taste in their mouths.

I just continued driving past the garden, not bothering to slow down or look.

Petty Annoyances

There are days when there are whole bunches of petty annoyances.

Used to be I really let them bother me.

Today I'm letting them slide off my back like water off a duck.

I find myself even laughing at that image.

I'm thankful today that I can do that. Laugh about things.

I just sort of go with the flow. It's just the way some days go.

I no longer have to say anything, get in the middle of it, or concern myself about it.

I keep my eyes and mind on a bigger picture. I've got better things to do with my time. And I am so grateful.

Today I ask myself if I will allow myself to trip over insignificant things until I'm no longer available to handle the really important things?

The answer is no.

I like being ready to handle the big stuff.

On Gossip and Spreading Negativity

I try not to listen to gossip.

I don't like hearing negative things about people anymore.

And I don't like thinking negative things about people either.

I like to keep my mind open to the positive things that people do and how they are.

I especially guard against my gossiping or saying something unkind about somebody to anybody else.

It's not fair to that person.

If I have a concern with someone, I prefer now to address it with them face-to-face.

Besides, I'm finding that when I think unkindly about people, it influences my words and actions towards them.

I can unconsciously say or do something negative.

And then I'd have to undo what I said or did, which I'd prefer not to have to do.

The damage would have been done already.

It's easier, and I prefer, to keep my thoughts and actions positive.

On Gossip and Spreading Negativity, Continued

I'm finding it to be true that when I have negative thoughts about someone, it eats away at me.

So, if I believe that someone has done something that wrong, I mentally try to forgive that person.

And if I've spoken with that person and cannot amicably resolve it, I try to avoid dealing with that person again.

I do it as politely as I can.

No need to fuel any more fires.

I wish the person well and move on in my relationships with other people.

Today, I choose to focus on positive thoughts and concerns, preferring to do it as quickly as possible.

I'd rather concentrate on the good things that I'd like to see happen, rather than the negative things that have happened.

Today, I keep my thoughts and activities as upbeat and hopeful as possible.

More on Gossip and Spreading Negativity

If I listen to negativity, chances are I will think and act negatively.

It might spoil an opportunity to participate in something good.

Today, I leave myself open to new and positive ideas and possibilities.

I don't want stumbling blocks or obstacles to get in the way.

Rumors and innuendos seem to do that.

Most times there are little to no truth to them; they're just somebody else's reactions or perceptions about people they don't like.

I prefer to form my own opinions based on my experiences.

And I'd rather work to be part of helping things along for the better—not creating blocks to potentially good solutions.

Or, joining forces with people who try to slander other people.

It's helpful situations I seek, not participating in hurting or denigrating others.

On Helping New People Feel Welcomed

When I join new groups, events, or worksites, I have found that few people go out of their way to welcome someone new.

I usually feel uncomfortable and think that people are acting "cliquish."

I think, this isn't for me.

Thank goodness, though, that I stayed for most things.

"Breaking the ice" is not easy.

I realize now that people's "cliquish-ness" is due to their own fears of talking to somebody new.

So, I've learned to step out of my comfort zone and break the ice myself.

I usually find people receptive when I do that, and it makes my experience much more pleasurable.

Now when I see somebody new, I make the effort to make them feel welcomed.

I remember what it's like to be in their shoes.

And I like knowing that I can make someone else feel welcomed.

On Breaking the Ice

It's hard to go someplace and not know anyone.

It's hard to strike up a conversation with a stranger.

I wonder what to say, my heart beats fast, I worry I'll stutter or sound silly.

The awkwardness can stop me right in my tracks.

However, the other person is usually as nervous as I am.

Somehow we get through those first moments.

And if it doesn't work, it's okay.

I take a deep breath, look at the other person sympathetically, and say something kindly like, "I'm going to get a cup of coffee. Nice meeting you though. I'll see you later, I'm sure."

Regaining my composure, I try again with someone else.

Usually, something will click—especially when one of us says "These events get me really nervous" and the other responds with "Me, too!"

We're off and running with a new quick friendship.

My Life's in Trust

An interesting thought crosses my mind from time to time.

My life may not be my own.

It may be a gift entrusted to me and it's my job to make as best use of it as I can.

The point of all this may be for me not to get what I can for myself, but to live my life in the best way possible to do what I can for others.

To do this, I need to listen to people, be supportive of them and try to be of use.

No matter how small the contribution, I need to try to make things better for everyone.

I don't want to break that trust today.

Treat the Whole Day Spiritually—Revisited

I try to treat the whole day spiritually like I do each morning, reading encouragements and reflecting.

With each new activity, I take a few breaths and clear my mind.

I focus my attention on listening to whoever is speaking, saying as little as possible—trying to fully grasp what they're relating.

I reserve any judgments about what they're saying, or about them, until later.

I remind myself to be grateful that they have shared their ideas with me, and I thank them for what they've had to say.

When I'm alone, I spend a few moments reviewing my reactions and judgments.

I mentally file them away, if need be, for further reflection at another time.

Then I take a quick break.

When the next activity begins, I'll clear my mind again, breathe deeply, and listen once more.

What a great way to spend the day.

When the End Comes

It's not easy to consider, but I wonder when the end comes, will I think *it went too fast?*

Will I be able to say that I savored my life as much as I could?

That I gave each day as much consideration as possible?

Will I be upset that I cannot take my material possessions with me?

Or, will I smile thinking how much I've given away and how much I have received in return?

Will I be grateful for this gift of life?

Or, will I be bitter thinking it didn't turn out how I wanted?

Will I have one more temper tantrum at the end— having not gotten my way?

Or, will I feel *it's all been good,* feeling satisfied and at peace?

Most of all, today's the day to live my life in a way to answer those questions affirmatively.

Tomorrow might be too late.

I'm Always Seeking Something

I'm always seeking something. Isn't that true for all of us?

I keep wanting this or that. I want more.

I want what you have.

I keep feeling like I'm missing something or something's missing in me.

I'm incomplete.

But that hole inside of me is getting filled.

That missing part is no longer missing as I encourage myself and reflect.

As I spend time thinking about what I have to offer and what I'd like to do.

As I sort through my emotions and clear my thinking.

As I'm helping the people I love, the people I'm close with or work with, these new acquaintances and folks who seem like they could use a hand.

These things are making me feel whole. Complete.

They fill me and fulfill me.

They make me focus on and appreciate how much I already have—*not on what I don't have or think that I still need.*

On Giving That Something a Name

So, I didn't create this world and this world is only one dot in a universe of infinite dots.

It's amazingly wondrous and overpowering to think about.

What is this force, this something, that brought all this into existence?

How did it happen?

And another powerful thought is trying to give that something a name.

If I name it, it becomes personal to me—a part of my life, an entity that I can relate to.

I can have a dialogue with it, using its name in a conversation, asking it for help.

Saying please and thank you to it. Relying on it. Knowing it's always there.

However important whatever it is that's upsetting me, when I consider the vast universe and this power that I have a name for, things seem to be put into perspective and I become calmer.

More About Toxic People

I try not to spend any more time than necessary with toxic people, and I try not to think poorly of them

When I do have to meet with them and if I begin to feel upset, I ask to take a break.

During that break, I use my tools to calm myself down, reminding myself that I'm getting too involved.

I remind myself to just listen as patiently as possible and consider how I can express myself in constructive ways.

I try to forgive them if they become highly negative and forgive myself any impatience I may have with them.

I try to finish my business quickly, without being rude.

And then I move on, knowing I did the best that I could, wishing them well, and doing whatever it is I need to do next.

A Short, Sweet and Simple Lesson in Acceptance

I have learned today that when I'm offered help, I can now say, "Yes, I can use some help. Thank you."

Today, I accept that help.

In fact, I've even learned to ask for it.

The Things That Still Haunt Me

From time to time, the past comes back to haunt me—whether in person or in memory.

Suddenly I feel some pang of guilt or embarrassment. Physically, I might tighten up, my heart might beat faster, I might feel anxious.

Whatever is haunting me is unresolved. I did something wrong, something I regret or still feel uncomfortable about.

So, I need to confront this ghost. I have to do something.

I reflect on it, considering what went wrong. I try to forgive myself and the people involved, decide if I can make it right, ask people I trust for their opinions about it, and then take some action to straighten it out.

It doesn't matter whether the other person accepts it or a particular situation changes as a result.

What matters is that I do my part to set it straight.

It's one less ghost around to still haunt me.

The Difficulties of Apologizing

When a memory is really uncomfortable, I cringe.

It's then I know I've done something very wrong.

I'm guilty.

So, I spend time thinking it over and deciding what I can do.

It's especially difficult when I think the other person started it or made it worse. When I believe the other person was wrong, deserved it, or had it coming—but none of that matters.

What matters is what I did.

What matters is that I need to straighten it out. Clean up my side of the street and stop focusing on the other person.

I need to apologize and make things right.

Even better than it was, if I can.

When I do that, I no longer cringe.

That feels much better.

Inadequacy, Disloyalty, and Confidence

When I'm not feeling up to a task or it when seems that someone is trying to make me feel that way, I try to recognize what is happening as quickly as possible.

I don't want to allow myself to feel inadequate—whether because of someone else or my own insecurities.

I've come to understand that when I allow myself to feel or be intimidated, I'm being disloyal to myself.

Why?

Because I'm pretty comfortable now believing that I'm capable.

So, I stop and reflect: why I am being disloyal to myself?

My self-confidence returns rather quickly.

What I'm doing may not work out perfectly, but ultimately it works out just fine.

In the Rush of Daily Living

In the rush of daily living, little things can get overlooked or left behind.

I can get too involved in what I think is so important.

It's then that I remember that I've forgotten to take time this morning to read my daily encouragement, to reflect and meditate, to feel grateful.

But here's an interesting thought.

I've come to realize that the power and strength that I have gotten in doing these things never leave me.

It's only me that leaves them behind.

So, when I remember what I've overlooked, which usually is my reliance on my daily discipline—I stop and start my day all over again.

It's never too late to do that.

And all the goodness and strength that I realized I was missing, is still there just waiting for me to pick up where I left off.

Here's a Suggestion—Sunshine!

There are days when encouragements and reflection don't seem to "cut it."

On those days I try other things to give myself a sense of inner peace.

I reach into my toolbox and try chanting, walking, dancing, exercising, or some other tool.

Sometimes I try—Sunshine!

If the weather is nice, I sit outside and turn my head upwards towards the sun.

I feel its warmth on my face, and it soon radiates throughout my body.

I feel like it's cleansing everything about me, including my heart and my spirit.

If it's cold outside, I sit by a window.

I feel the heat of the sun coming through it and I welcome how good it makes me feel.

On a rainy or overcast day, I visualize the sun and a wonderfully warm blanket around me.

So, teasingly I say to you, "Try it, Sunshine!"

Playing Catch

Fear can immobilize me.

I fear doing something imperfectly and you'll criticize or humiliate me.

But these are my own fears about failing.

I project them onto you.

It's safer to blame you.

I'm not hurting me, you are. I'm a victim.

I need to stop this. I'm not a victim and I need to stop fearing failure.

So, I have a tool I use:

I imagine reaching into my head, pulling these fears out and throwing them up to this spiritual entity, this divine force.

I play "catch."

I say to that entity, "Here. Take my fears from me. I don't want them anymore. I need them to stop."

Sometimes I have to play "catch" several times, but it works.

I don't want to self-bully anymore.

I don't want to project my fears onto someone else.

I can own them now and I can get rid of them.

Another Way to Fight Self-Bullying

My self-bullying has to stop.

Every time I doubt myself or worry about being humiliated, I imagine throwing these thoughts into the "garbage dump of the universe."

I don't want them anymore.

I am, and always have been, alright.

I've made mistakes, but none of them are worth how badly I beat myself over them.

Today I say a sort of prayer.

I ask that my self-doubting be taken from me, that I will be filled with self-peace and a quiet confidence.

I ask to feel comfortable participating constructively in the day ahead.

And I express gratitude for receiving the help I need to change.

I repeat it often when I start to bully myself.

I've written it down, so I remember. It helps.

I am changing.

Looking Inward to Move Outward

I look inward now to move outward.

Sounds silly, right?

Makes perfect sense to me.

When I look outward, I'm only seeing what's in front of me.

My mind usually goes into judgment mode, thinking:

What's that? Is it good or bad? Do I need it?

Do I like it? Should I take it? Should I get rid of it?

Can I change it? Can I make it better? Different?

But when I look inward, I feel things, sense things.

I observe. I watch.

I'm not judging or questioning or manipulating but feeling an inner peace and what's right for me.

So, I've stopped looking only outwardly and spend time now looking inwardly, so I can live more comfortably outwardly.

Got that?

A Source of Strength

I've met many people who tell me that they rely on daily reflecting and encouragements.

They tell me the same thing: It gives them a sense of peacefulness.

They don't see their reliance on it as a weakness. Instead, they see it as a strength.

It seems that when something is practiced regularly, it makes that person stronger.

But the strength that comes from this practice, this discipline, is that sense of peacefulness—and of belonging.

It's paradoxical to think of peacefulness and belonging as strength.

Most times we think of strength as trying to be stronger than someone or something.

In a way, we are doing just that. We are overcoming ourselves.

I am overcoming my doubts and fears, and developing more ability to think things through, to act constructively, to persevere, and to have hope.

What a comfort and strength that is.

Stop Making Myself Angry

I make myself angry about the same things day after day.

For example, traffic is always bumper-to-bumper and takes forever. And every day I fume, honk and yell.

Why? How is that helping me?

Today I will act differently.

Instead of getting angry, I will try something new.

I will listen to music, think about what's good in the world, or I will call someone.

I will stop at a store or a restaurant on the way home. Maybe I will call someone to meet me there.

I'll take a different route and enjoy a change of scenery.

I'll consider moving closer to work, moving somewhere with less traffic, consider a ride share, or see if I can change my work hours.

But getting angry, over and over again, at the same things every day only eats away at me.

I need to make changes.

I'm Finding It Important to Talk with Others

As I'm changing, I like discussing what I'm discovering with some of the people around me.

I'm finding it important, as well as comforting, to open up a little with people that I trust, or am coming to trust.

I talk about how disillusioned I used to be and how every little thing used to get me.

How high I would set expectations for myself, and for everyone else.

How this used to really get in my way, being irritable so much of the time.

I talk about how I now practice daily reflection and read encouragements, trying to find new ways of perceiving situations and reacting to them.

It's comforting to let others know that I'm trying to change and become more willing to be supportive of everyone around me.

I usually feel good afterward. I'm much more comfortable sharing myself with others now.

I Need a Sense of Comfort

Everyone needs a sense of comfort, to feel safe and secure.

I've always wanted it, but I was too busy bouncing off walls, making myself feel insecure.

Each day now has an opportunity for me to feel that sense of comfort.

But I have to provide it to myself.

I wrap an imaginary blanket of reassurance around my shoulders, so that I feel safe and comforted throughout the day.

If I put myself into a position in which I might have to worry about how I'm acting or how others might react to me, I stop and think, *Do I really need to get into this right now?*

And then I answer myself with a resounding, *No!*

I pull that imaginary blanket of reassurance around my shoulders, comfort myself, and feel good that I didn't let myself bounce off the walls once again.

On Battling and Resting

My old routines had me tired and beaten down because I made so many things a battle.

Lately though, I'm able to step back from whatever's going on and remind myself that I don't have to get into the middle of everything.

When I step back, I rest and think about something else.

I take my mind off of the immediate frustrations that I'm feeling.

After I take that break and take some deep breaths, when I do return to the situation that's confronting me, I'm feeling calm and ready to see what I can do to help—rather than doing battle.

And if I get frustrated once more, I'll just take another break.

This practice of resting, taking a break, really helps.

The Clerk and I

I recently needed a store clerk to assist me.

But I thought the clerk wasn't being helpful, and we were both getting heated.

The thought crossed my mind that my getting angry wasn't going to make things any better.

I stopped, inhaled, and relaxed for a moment.

I looked at the clerk and said, I'm sorry. This is getting a little heated. I know you're only doing your job.

I then added, I imagine you've been in situations like this yourself, and I wonder what you've done.

The clerk's mood immediately changed.

She stopped too, thought about it, and then began to offer me her experience.

It became a helpful conversation and turned a situation of antagonism into cooperation.

Better things happen when I step back, take a breath, and relax.

Today I try to practice this as often as I can.

Surprise!

I'm realizing that to be a part of life, I have to be in it.

I can't sit on the sidelines and throw stones. Nor can I stand over it, looking down at everyone and yelling at them.

First, I have to decide for myself what I'd like, and stop focusing on what everybody else is doing wrong.

Once I can focus on what I'd like, I can then begin to participate in the process.

When I get a dialogue going, I'm feeling like I'm a part of what's going on.

I'm coming to understand that I won't necessarily get the answers that I want, but I'll feel better just by airing my concerns.

And by listening to other people's ideas—instead of criticizing them—I might find out that what they have to suggest is better than what I thought was good.

What a surprise!

Everything in Its Own Time and Place, Including Me

I'm realizing how important it is to recognize that everything has its own time and place.

The world turns in place at its own speed. And I have to stop trying to speed it up or slow it down. The truth is I can't do anything about it.

All I can do is decide if I want to jump in or not. And if I do jump in, for how long? Or if I decide to stay out, how long can I stay out for?

The same is true for events and people.

They all go at their own speeds and in their own places.

I'm observing my own speed and place in everything, and trying to move at a more consistent speed and in a comfortable place—not going at a breakneck speed or refusing to move at all.

It's a learning experience.

Beginning and Practicing

Each day begins anew.

And I begin it by asking for help, reflecting, being grateful, and thinking about the day ahead.

I mentally practice how I want to be during the day.

If I put this off, then I seem to put everything off during the day.

And I only wind up being put off too.

I don't want to live like that anymore.

I don't want to put things off, I don't want to be put off and I don't want to live on the edge.

By practicing patience, focusing on what I might want and talking about it, by being ready to compromise or at least listen to what other people have to say, my day goes a lot better.

But it has to start that way first thing in the morning.

I have to begin it by practicing.

Crackpot, Hotshot, or Good-Shot: Undersized, Oversized, or Rightsized?

I can spend my time being a crackpot: being balmy, batty, bonkers, mad, maniacal, nutty, or unhinged.

I can also spend my time being a hotshot: feeling super important, like I know better, making other people feel less, criticizing, and wanting my own way.

Lately, I prefer just to recognize my talents and abilities, fitting in, trying to be poised, participating along with everyone else, and contributing what I can.

I tend to think of that as spending my time being a good-shot. I like that idea a lot better.

I no longer have to or want to denigrate my abilities nor overvalue them either.

I just have to find the right balance for me, being rightsized.

More Helping Others

Lately, I've had opportunities to help others who are going through difficult times.

I've been finding it to be helpful for me as I'm listening more than talking.

I try to be sympathetic as well as encouraging.

If I have something to share from my own life, I share it.

I talk about similar experiences that I've had and how they have affected me.

I ask them what they're doing to cope with what they're going through.

Then I listen some more.

I might share how I'm coping too.

I ask them if what they're doing is working for them.

I listen again.

Then, I let it go.

I've offered whatever help I can by sharing my own experiences and what I do.

Maybe, I've even heard something from them that I can try myself.

When I Can't Sleep, I Can Laugh

There are nights when I just can't sleep. I worry and obsess.

I think how ridiculous it is that I keep thinking the same thoughts over and over.

So, I practice some breathing, I meditate or chant a while, I count sheep backward from 100, I drink chamomile or sleepy time tea, or I play calming background sounds like rain or chimes.

The most important thing I do is not letting myself get upset over it.

I try to laugh at my obsessiveness.

Eventually, I do fall asleep.

And when I wake up, I make light of it, laughing at my "runaway mind."

Then I get on with my day, not losing any sleep over my lack of sleep. Ha.

And I'm grateful for what I do have: a new day today and maybe a good night's sleep tonight.

Always Seeking Something

Never Fails

So much in life fails.

I'm not being negative or pessimistic. But it's true.

However, taking time each morning to read encouragements and reflect never seems to fail.

As I practice these things, embracing what I've come to see as spiritual principles, and sheltering myself within them, the outcomes become less important.

It is not a matter of whether something succeeds or fails, it is the fact that I am comfortable with who I am, what I'm trying to do, and whether what I'm doing is good, helpful, and caring.

The outcome is not the important thing.

The thought and action are.

That never fails.

What Others Think

I understand now that when I worry about what other people think of me, I'm really only projecting my own thoughts about myself onto them.

It's easier to imagine people judging or criticizing me than to accept the fact that I'm judging or criticizing myself.

The truth is I really don't know what other people are thinking.

I do know what I'm thinking.

So, I need to use my thoughts constructively and not project them onto somebody else.

Today I ask myself: am I truly trying to be helpful? Do I mean well? Am I expecting too much? Am I being fair?

If my intentions are good, I don't need to worry about the outcome.

If my intentions aren't good and I'm just being self-centered, then I need to adjust my thinking and my actions.

Pretty simple, just not easy.

A Checklist for Progress

I like to review how I'm progressing.

I ask myself:

- Am I less sensitive about things?
- Do I take a break when I'm getting upset?
- How much time do I actually spend listening?
- Do I go out of my way to help someone?
- How well do I face up to my mistakes?
- Do I allow myself to recognize the good things that I do too?
- How grateful do I really feel for what I have?

I try to be as honest with myself as possible, and where I'm doing well, recognize it for myself.

If I cringe at a question, then I spend time reflecting on what and why I might be avoiding.

I don't do this perfectly, but I do it as perfectly as I can.

I ask myself, have I accepted that it's progress that I'm really after.

Failing Does Not Mean I'm a Failure

I've come to realize that if I tried something and it failed, it doesn't mean that I'm a failure.

It just means that it didn't work out.

The goal may have been set too high, the environment wasn't conducive, more time was needed, the anticipated help or resources weren't available, I lost interest, or so on.

These are not excuses, these are realities.

Usually, when I try something, I can achieve it. But realistically, it doesn't always happen.

When I evaluate the so-called "failure," it really means that I'm looking at what happened in a reasonable light.

I try to treat the undertaking, as well as myself and the others who might have been involved, in a respectful and understanding way.

Everyone tries their best to succeed. Even me.

Everything I Need, I Already Have

Sometimes it seems like I'm missing things.

It seems like I'm missing out on something in life, I'm missing out on something I wanted, I'm missing the help that I need, and so on.

But when I stop and reflect, when I take the time each morning to think about what it is I think I'm missing—I realize that either: I already have it or I don't really need it or I'm capable of working towards having it.

So today I try to stay focused on what I have, what I've gotten, and what I can do.

Not what I'm missing.

The Two Main Ingredients in Life

Each day as I reflect, life seems to get a little simpler.

I'm beginning to see that the two main ingredients in my life today are: to love and to create.

And when I'm loving, I'm able to create. And when I'm creating, I'm doing it with love.

Everything else seems to flow from that.

If it's not, then I'm not being loving or creative.

Most likely, I'm being overly judgmental of myself or others, and allowing fear to take over.

Today I don't want the criticisms or fears.

I'll try to stick with the other two main ingredients.

When Things Go Up or Down

When things are going well, I need to be careful not to think that it will always be that way.

I take things for granted then, and also begin to think it's going well all because of me.

Yes, my life is better because of the things I'm doing to make it better.

But life has its own cycles of ups and downs, and it doesn't depend on me.

When life gets difficult, I also need to be careful not to think that it will always be that way too.

I also need to remember that when things aren't going well, it's not because I'm doing something wrong.

That's not true either.

Life just changes.

My job is to keep myself as consistent as I can be.

My Idea of Perfect

I keep imagining everything would be perfect if only this or that would happen.

I plan on making everything perfect. I obsess about it.

If only you would listen and do things the way I want them to be done.

And when it doesn't happen that way, I get upset.

I don't like your ideas and what you want.

So, nothing is perfect because I don't accept things as they are.

That's a real slap in the face.

I've come to realize that what I want is only my own personal vision. Nobody else necessarily shares that vision. In fact, few people even care whether something is perfect or not.

Most people just want to enjoy themselves.

Slowly, I'm getting to that point myself.

And when I can do that, just enjoy myself, everything seems to be pretty perfect.

I Need a Little Action

Although I get so much from daily encouragements and reflecting, I realize that I also have to do something.

I have to take some action.

Keeping my thoughts and emotions in balance is important, but I find it more helpful when I do something for someone else.

It reinforces for me that I'm doing okay and living life on a better footing.

So today, I do simple things like holding a door open for someone, letting another driver get in the lane in front of me, or paying for the coffee for the person in line who is fumbling for change.

That's the easy stuff.

The harder stuff is doing things at work or at home without being asked, and doing it without telling anyone.

But, wow . . .

It's amazing what it does for me!

Always Seeking Something

It seems like I'm always seeking something.

Like I want more, something else, something you have and I don't.

Reading encouragements and reflecting helps me realize that I already have most of what I want.

And what I might be missing, I can find by joining various groups, attempting new things, and talking with different people.

These activities help me to feel complete.

There is another thing that I have found too.

The realization that there is this force or power that exists that is greater than me, greater than all of us.

This spiritual entity or energy fills me with a sense of gratitude and inspires me.

As I reflect on it, I don't feel like I need to seek much else.

I feel satisfied, I belong here—where I am and with what I have.

My Views About Today Depend on Me

If I'm already tired in the morning when I reflect, I might worry about being exhausted as the day wears on.

If I'm already feeling upset, I might fret that I'll feel upset all day.

If I'm feeling somewhat anxious, I can obsess about becoming more anxious later.

My mood and my thinking, first thing in the morning, can affect how I think my day will go.

It's true.

So, rather than focus on my mood and how it might affect my day, I reflect on what I anticipate doing today and how I will enjoy being part of it.

I reflect on participating, doing the best I can and being grateful that I can join in.

How my day will be is not dependent on how I might be feeling at any given moment.

Moods change.

My ability to participate, doing my best, and being grateful does not.

The Creation of Things

When I reflect on the fact that I did not create this world and that this world is only one tiny dot in a universe of infinite dots, I feel an immense feeling of awe.

How did all this come into existence and what continues to hold it all together?

I am absolutely mind-boggled by it.

There is this amazing force, an unknowable constant, which people refer to by many names: God, Buddha, Jesus, Allah, the Tao, Higher Power, Divine Principle, and so on.

As I reflect on it, I feel grounded.

I gain a spiritual and realistic perspective.

Whatever may be disturbing me, when I consider how all of this came into being, is lessened in significance.

There are more important things in the world than what might be on my mind.

Begin and Practice

Two important words: begin and practice.

Every day I have an opportunity to begin anew.

I reflect and I encourage myself.

I think about the day ahead and helpful ways for me to participate in it.

I do this every day. It's a matter of practice.

The more I practice, the easier it becomes.

But if I put it off, my days tend not to go as well, and it becomes more difficult to get back into a practice.

If I miss a day, I stop and begin again.

The reality is that I can begin my day again at any time during that same day.

It works when I begin, and it begins when I practice.

It has to start somewhere.

Pretty simple stuff.

Beginning and practicing.

Blink!

I like to think that I have control over my life.

That I can influence things, at least to a certain degree.

But ultimately, many things are completely out of my control.

Thinking that I have the ability to make choices makes me feel good—like I'm in charge.

But much of life happens on its own.

I struggle with that.

I want so much to feel like I'm in control.

This morning I reflected on this thought: Blink!

It became an analogy for me about life.

Before I can even realize it, like a blink, something will change.

That put things into a pretty powerful perspective for me.

It reminds me to enjoy what I have at this moment to the best of my ability.

It makes me forget about control.

It reminds me to be grateful—right now!

And to enjoy what I have right now.

What's Up With That?

So, I can't have a temper tantrum when I don't get my own way?

I can't sit around all day, or even all week, feeling self-pity?

You're telling me that I can't complain to everyone around me about how bad things are?

I can't tell you to your face how wrong you are and where you need to go?

Then, what's left for me?

You tell me to lower my expectations of everyone—and myself.

You tell me not to take on more than I can handle, to relax, and take things in stride.

You tell me to think things through and to talk with people about what I might like.

You really know how to spoil a party!

And now I'm supposed to be happy, giving, and grateful because of all that?

Huh!

Tell me, what's up with that?

True Charity

Am I charitable?

I don't mean throwing loose change into a donation can.

Or writing checks to some charitable organization.

Everyone does that.

And I'm not knocking it. It's a good thing.

What I'm talking about is being charitable in my heart.

- Do I allow for others' mistakes and failures?
- Can I look the other way when it happens?
- Can I let someone know that I've done the same thing?
- Can I stand by them and help them?

How compassionate and understanding am I?

That's the charity I'd like to have.

And, how nice! Because the way I'm treating others is the way I find they are treating me in return.

So, kindness does seem to beget kindness.

And I'm beginning to treat myself with the same kindness that I'm treating others with—and what a difference that's making for me too.

A Subtle Laughable Insight

Here's my logical mind at work:

Some days I swear that I am not making headway.

Then I think I am not making headway because I am not taking all of this in.

Then it occurs to me that if I could take all of this in, I wouldn't need to keep reading all of this because I was taking it all in.

Then it made sense to me why I keep reading all of this.

What's Really Important?

Sometimes I start to do something but decide in the meanwhile that something else is more important to do first.

Then, after doing that, I start again on what I wanted to do, only to find again that there is something else I need to do before I can finish the first thing I wanted to do.

Sometimes this goes on all day long.

Seems like maybe throughout my entire life. *Ha!*

So, what's really important?

Sometimes I think the answer is *whatever is in front of me at that moment* is what's important.

But even then, something else might become more important.

Even more important than what I thought was important initially.

Then again, who's to judge?

Another *Ha!*

How important is anything, really?

In Plain English—Why Ain't It Perfect?

Some days I'm so frustrated with this process of reflecting and encouragements that I laugh and call it deflecting and discouragements.

That's because bad things still happen.

As I practice this daily discipline, shouldn't everything be perfect? At least be better?

You would think so, right? I mean, isn't that why I'm doing this?

But everything is better. I just don't always see it that way.

And when I don't, it's because I'm not getting what I want or life isn't happening the way I planned it.

For example, people shouldn't die, natural disasters shouldn't happen, my boss shouldn't have reprimanded me, my toast shouldn't have burnt, and so on.

But life happens.

My daily encouragements help me find ways to cope with it, accept it the way it is and find acceptable ways to respond.

As I get better at doing that, life gets better.

Even almost perfect.

Curses

When I curse at traffic, when I curse my boss, curse my sports team's best player for an error, curse a family member for being lackadaisical, curse a rainy day interfering with my plans, I am really cursing myself.

I only make things worse when I see life not as it is, but how I insist it should be—the way I want it to be.

If I am grateful throughout the day, no matter how frustrating things become, I can see life as it is and work my way through it.

Big difference.

Not that difficult to do, actually.

Criticism

Criticism doesn't work; neither self-criticism nor criticizing someone else.

It only leads to anger, defensiveness, and disappointment.

I need to look at what I want and consider how I might get there without stepping on someone else's toes.

I need to remember that what you want and what I want may be very different.

Even the ways we attempt to achieve them may differ and we may need to change as we move forward.

Criticizing each other won't work.

The key here is accepting change.

If we are flexible and adaptable, then we can discuss things and we'll be okay.

So, I reflect on how willing am I to change as I move ahead?

How willing am I to accept your changing too?

How flexible and adaptable can I be?

Can I remain positive and hopeful as we move forward, accepting changes as best I can?

It Is What It Is

How many times have I beaten myself up because I thought something I did wasn't perfect?

Wasn't good enough?

How many times have I stopped myself from trying something because of the fear of not doing something perfectly?

I've had to give up this notion of perfection.

The world isn't perfect: it's too hot, it's too cold, there's a drought, a flood, a fire, and so on.

Things happen.

They may seem bad or imperfect but they are also the natural order of things.

What I do, how much or how little, is up to me.

But it's never going to be perfect, and I don't have to beat myself up for it not being perfect.

Nor do I have to deny myself satisfaction because of it—or stop myself out of fear.

Today, I will do my best to be a part of the natural order of things.

Giving Up

I can read every encouragement that has ever been written but the necessary ingredient for all this to work is to "give up."

What the heck does that even mean?

It means I have to stop fighting everyone, to admit that I can't always "beat the system," that I might actually be powerless over most things, that much of the time I don't even manage my own life very well.

It means that unless and until I ask for help, and I become willing to take it—nothing will change.

I have to quit the "I know what's best for me and you and everybody else" club and ask to be admitted to the "I can't do this alone and I want all the help I can get" club.

Do I give up perfectly?

No. Not even close.

But I do try every day to give up.

Share Humanity, Share Experience

I've come to realize that I don't know any more than anyone else.

But I also don't know a lot less than anyone else either.

What I have to share is what I've been through—my experience.

I can't tell you what's right or wrong, or what's for the best or not.

I don't know what's best for me often enough.

But I do know that I care.

That I want the best for you and for me.

I do know that I'm trying my best, and I know what's worked for me at times and what has not worked for me at other times.

And when I talk with you, this is what I try to share.

And I hope when you talk with me that you share the same in exchange.

It's what makes us human.

But I didn't always realize this.

Mistakes? Give Me A Break!

There have been times when I thought: I might make a mistake, so why try?

Chances are I might.

So what?

I've come to realize that when I make a mistake, I can think *Ugh*, and move on.

I don't know why I make such a big deal out of trying to do something without making a mistake.

Why do I get so worried about it?

I know now that I can just say, *oh well, I tried*, and do it over or do something else.

There will always be a next time. Always another time.

And there will always be those past successes that I've had too.

Nothing is lost.

60 Seconds

I read that Ralph Waldo Emerson once wrote:

> *For every minute that you are angry, you lose sixty seconds of happiness.*

That made me laugh.

The obviousness of it struck me funny.

Then my face dropped.

Because when I thought about it, I realized it wasn't just seconds.

For me, it was days at a time.

I had spent a good deal of my life being angry.

And I also wasted time living in fear, beating myself up, withdrawing, obsessing, and on many other emotions.

All that time that I could have been enjoying myself and everybody around me.

Today I don't want to waste a minute.

We Are Who We Are

When I'd see people with better jobs, nicer cars, bigger houses—I'd think, *why not me?*

Today I think it's realistic to feel a little envious from time to time, but I also think *what I have today is pretty darn good too.*

Could it be better? Sure.

But it could be worse too.

So, I remain grateful for what I do have.

I see people who seem worse off than me.

I think, *there but for the grace of God, go I.*

Yet some of them seem just as happy, if not happier than I am.

I'm realizing that possessions are not what make people happy.

It's how I perceive what I have and what I do with it.

As I become more satisfied with myself, because of what I'm doing, I appreciate how much I have gotten already—and how much I keep getting.

"The-Hell-With-It" Syndrome

I have a problem that I call "The-Hell-With-It" syndrome.

It happens when little things pile up and I reach a breaking point, saying, "The hell with it."

Then I do things I know I shouldn't do, like: blowing up at people, overeating, sulking, and generally engaging in self-defeating behaviors.

I even get that self-pitying syndrome called, "Who-Even-Cares!"

But I'm training myself to remember, before ever reaching that point, that I care, and I don't want to lose what I've worked so hard for.

I don't want to pull the house down on top of me and everyone I care about.

So, I stop, ask for help of some sort or another, and begin to think things through.

In simpler terms, I take a break right then and there. I clear my mind.

I care too much to undo all that I've tried to build up.

Going South

Here's a simple truth: Nothing gets better if I don't try to make it better.

Pretty basic stuff.

If I don't at least try, then things will, most likely, go south.

I'm not talking about changing the world.

I'm talking about making one change, even a small one, generally within myself.

Usually the change I need involves how I'm perceiving what's happening around me.

If I won't at least try to change my perception, how I can evaluate something differently—I guarantee things will get worse.

I'll harbor a grudge, stomp my feet, and make everyone, including myself, miserable.

And things will then go south that much faster.

Playing

Someone recently suggested that I try to "play more."

It was suggested that I try acting like a kid again.

Have fun. Be silly.

Forget about worrying what other people might think and just enjoy myself.

Find the child within me. The kid I used to be.

Laugh more, especially at myself. Not take things so seriously.

It was suggested that I remember how I played at playgrounds, running around, getting sweaty, playing tag, laughing, and teasing other kids, going swimming and doing cannonballs off of diving boards, and just having a great time.

It was suggested that I give myself permission to enjoy being that kid again.

So, today, and I've been doing this for a while now, I play.

I have some fun.

I don't take myself so seriously.

I Need a Daily Refill

What I learned yesterday, I may not remember today.

What I learn today, I may not remember tomorrow.

The same may be true for the day after.

It's not that I'm stupid. I'm human.

I'm like the fire that goes out unless more wood is added.

Like the car that needs the accelerator stepped on in order to move forward.

Like the water jug that needs refilling.

Every day I need wood to be added, my accelerator stepped on and my jug refilled.

It's no big deal.

It's all routine.

Every day I read, I reflect, and I practice.

On Waiting and Watching

A difficult thing for me to do is wait and watch.

I often rush into things, make changes, and tell people what to do.

When I do that, I find myself in the thick of things, causing people to react strongly to me.

I get in so deep that I can't see the forest from the trees.

I can create a lot of chaos.

In fact, I am the chaos.

Slowly, I'm learning to wait and watch what's going on.

Then, I can recognize what I might have to offer, what part to play, or whether I need to do anything at all.

Over time, I've found that many things simply work themselves out on their own—if I wait patiently and watch.

I'm even seeing things work out better than what I would have wanted or expected.

Imagine that!

Seeking Signs

Many people want a sign to let them know if what they're doing is right.

They want some external affirmation or approval.

But what if you don't get one?

Or worse yet, what if you missed it because you were preoccupied—will you get a second one?

Are there second chances with signs?

Of course, I'm teasing.

I'm coming to rely on that quiet reassurance inside of me that comes with daily reflection.

I consider what I need to do today, which usually is to wait, watch and decide what, if anything, I might sensibly be able to contribute.

Signs are nice, but I don't think they're necessary.

Or, even reasonable.

Plus, if I expect one, I might get disappointed if I don't get it or I miss it.

I'd rather look within myself for answers than for a shooting star.

Can't Remind Myself Enough About This

In the middle of change, the best thing I can do is to remain calm.

When everyone else is shouting, the best thing I can do is listen.

When everyone else is ruffled, including me, I need to sit tight.

The best thing I can do is give myself time, treat the situation with kindness and wait.

By getting involved too quickly, I will be reacting rather than being helpful.

I'll probably upset everyone, including myself, and then want to extract myself from the situation as quickly as possible.

Here's the question: Why do that to myself and everyone else?

If I give myself time, and that's one thing that I can control, the dust will most likely settle and things may work themselves out.

So, I remind myself: Do nothing.

Which is actually something.

Which is a great paradox which usually now works in my favor.

Treat Every Day as if it's Friday

I love this expression: treat every day as if it's the end of your workweek.

We all know how it feels when we realize, "It's Friday!"

We're suddenly happy that the week of tension is about to be over.

But I'm learning to treat every day as if it was Friday.

I'm realizing that all my angst exists in my mind, not in the day of the week.

No one is wasting as much of their time worrying about me as I am.

So, I need to quit.

If I begin to worry, I stop and spend a little time reflecting on what change I can make and then I start to do it.

When I'm done, I remind myself that it's Friday.

Even if it isn't, it is.

Whoo-whoo.

Now tell me—what's really important?

Read This Line Over and Over Again

I told a friend of mine who practices meditation that I had trouble clearing my mind when I meditated.

He said it wasn't necessary to clear my mind as much as it was to just observe my thoughts as they crossed my mind.

He said it might be simpler, though, to just read this, and then he handed me the following:

> *I am reading this same line over and over.*
>
> *I am reading this same line over and over.*
>
> *I just keep reading it.*
>
> *As I read it, I'm breathing in and out.*
>
> *I'm only paying attention to the line and to my breathing—nothing else.*
>
> *I am reading this same line over and over again.*

Funny. It really helped.

I learned that it didn't take a whole lot to distance myself from my thoughts and outside distractions.

I just needed to read. And maybe breathe a little too.

All Work and No Reflection

I've had periods where I have had unlimited stamina.

I just kept going and going and going.

And then bam!

I exhausted myself.

Everything came crashing down. Grinding to a halt.

All I could do then was sleep.

I've learned that I can't keep going at full speed like that.

I need rest periods and breaks.

I've had to train myself to stop. It's not something that comes naturally.

Conversely, I've had periods where I was so filled with fear that I didn't want to do any work at all.

Ultimately, what I'm trying to do is to maintain a level playing field in which I don't keep going at full speed believing I can handle the entire world or avoiding the world fearing it will all be too much.

Like that little train, I know I can—but I have to do it at a reasonable pace.

The "Oh Well" Adaptation

I've been reflecting lately on my expectations of things.

I realize that I always have some expectations.

It's how hard I hold on to them that can deeply affect me.

Today, I try to think of them as simply hopes or dreams.

Things that I might look forward to, if possible.

I understand that life will happen no matter what I'd like to see happen.

I work towards certain things, but as the saying goes, *it will be what it will be.*

Sometimes I'm happy with the outcome, sometimes not.

But I try to mold my expectations to be as reasonable and realistic as possible, and I prepare myself for either outcome.

I've learned that there's nothing wrong with an "Oh well" response to disappointment and moving on to the next thing.

In fact, the "Oh well" response and then shrugging my shoulders work rather well.

The Person Who Doesn't Need to Speak

One goal of daily reflection and encouragement is to level out my life.

To live it as calmly and peacefully as possible.

I do that by trying to accept who and what I am.

I once read that the person who can do this seldom needs to speak.

Obviously, that's not me.

But the point is that you don't need to speak if you're content with who you are and accept that everything happens as it's going to happen.

That person may have emotional reactions to life's situations but understands that these responses pass.

I doubt that I'll ever reach that point of acceptance.

But I am striving to live in a way so that my reactions are not so extreme, keeping my life as even-keeled as possible.

Now that's a reasonable and realistic goal.

Is There a Heaven or Hell?

I recently heard a story about a minister who was asked if there really is a heaven or hell.

The clergyman said that everything indicates that there is.

The congregant asked, *But what do you believe, father?*

The priest gave the usual answer, *It's up to you to decide, and not for me to tell you what to believe.*

This went back and forth a few times until the parishioner got upset with the cleric and said, *What's the matter with you, father? Why can't you answer a simple question? Are you deaf or stupid?*

The answer he received from the clergyman was,

> *Now this has become hell.*

The question really is not whether there is a heaven or hell, but who creates it, and how?

Life Is Like a Football Game

When I think about it, life is like a football game. Ha!

I huddle, listen to the play, line up, concentrate on the signals, then either block, run, fake, tackle or catch, and then huddle up again.

Sometimes I'm called out to sit on the sidelines a while and rest.

Other times while I'm on the bench, I yell at the other team, cheer on my teammates, or just chat with them.

I get excited when the plays are made and disappointed when they aren't.

If my team wins, I feel great.

If we lose, I remind myself that we'll do better the next time.

I can also analyze the plays and learn from the experience.

But mostly I enjoy each game for what it's worth, just like I enjoy each day for what it's worth.

It's not a bad way to live.

Avoiding Daily Encouragements and Reflections

There have been times when I just didn't feel like reading encouragements or reflecting.

I'd feel rebellious and would question, *why do I need it?*

Or, I felt irritated that it wasn't working fast enough.

Or, it took up too much of my time, especially in the mornings.

Someone suggested that I just relax. That it was okay to take a break.

It was a good suggestion. Because pressuring myself never does me any good.

Once I took a break, I started back rather quickly.

I realized that when I avoided it for too long, I would find myself irritable again and remember how good I felt when I took the time each day to reflect.

So, I now know that I can give myself a break when I need one but I won't stay away for very long.

Even the Nastiest Person Becomes Nicer

As I take time each day to read encouragements and reflect, I'm so much more relaxed and at peace.

I think about what I can do to help other people. What I can do for them.

I'm finding that as I help others, and remain calm and supportive myself, they are reacting in the same calm and supportive manner too.

I know it's because I'm *acting* differently.

I'm no longer being selfish and as moody as I used to be.

And I'm surprised how nice the nastiest people have become.

Imagine that. Ha!

Why Do We Expect Certain Things?

One of my neighbors told me a story about how they were helping another neighbor who was going through a hard time.

They'd stop by every day to bring some food, a newspaper, or just to say hello.

After a while, the neighbor wasn't expressing appreciation anymore for these little acts of kindness.

So, the neighbor stopped being helpful.

I only know this because that neighbor gossiped to me about how ungrateful the other neighbor was.

It was a good lesson for me to think about.

When I do something nice for someone, do I need to get recognition in return?

If I don't get recognition, do I need to gossip about it?

The question really is: Can I be kind just to be kind?

Recognizing Stop Signs

As time goes by, I'm recognizing that I am becoming less impulsive.

I'm less prone to anger or to making snap judgments.

I know it's because I take time each day to read encouragements and reflect.

I'm learning to take deep breaths in certain situations, slow things down, and think things through.

When I'm in a tense encounter, I now think, *everyone is doing the best that they can.*

It's not that *I don't get* angry or *don't want* to express my opinion immediately, but I now hear this little voice in my head saying, *Wait!*

Sometimes I see a little light in my mind's eye going from green to yellow and then red.

I know it's time to quit then.

I also feel that knot in my throat or that tightness in my belly telling me to back off.

Funny how I never recognized these stop signs before.

The Gifts That I Have Been Given

Every day I'm realizing all the gifts I've been receiving lately as I act differently.

For example, I'm handling stress calmly, I'm enjoying being around people, people are asking me for help (imagine that!), I look around me and feel at peace, and so much more.

I'm putting in the work, but these results, these amazing gifts, are not coming from me.

They're coming from something well beyond me.

It feels like some power, some entity, because I am paying attention to how I'm acting, is rewarding me with presents that I never could have expected.

And I am so grateful.

What is happening is humbling—and powerful.

I am awed by all these gifts that I am receiving.

What a great turn my life has taken.

Sorting Myself Out

I'm finding that my emotions sometimes get intermixed with one another.

For example, sometimes when I express appreciation to someone, I also feel envious.

I can express regret for what I said to someone, and still feel a sense of superiority over them.

I can feel sorry for someone who is hurting yet feel pleasure knowing they're hurting.

It's important to recognize when these feelings coexist.

These hidden feelings, the ones that I don't express, can get communicated unconsciously and I end up hurting someone.

So, when I'm feeling envious of someone, I need to recognize that I'm successful in my own right.

When I'm feeling superior, I need to recognize that I don't know better than anyone else.

When I gloat over somebody who's hurting, I need to remember, *There but for the grace of God, go I.*

When I sort myself out, I hurt people a lot less.

Once Upon a Time

Once upon a time, someone was having a terrible day.

The car that wouldn't start and had to be towed, arriving late to work the boss was in a foul mood and found several mistakes in a project, an argument with a coworker ensued, and then a friend called upset by something that happened the day before.

However, at lunchtime, that person focused on their breathing, cleared their mind, and read some encouragements.

When that person left the restaurant, they noticed how many birds were straddling a branch of a tree, how fresh the air smelled, and how warm the sun was on their face.

For the moment, the person was filled with gratitude.

It no longer mattered how bad the morning was or whether the day would continue to be bad.

For that person, who was me, right then everything was perfect.

That was a new experience.

Practice, Practice, Practice

The "Letting Go by Throwing It Away" Tool

When a problem or situation becomes too overwhelming, I "let it go."

But before I do that, I reflect on it, talk about it with others, ask for help, and if it's still frustrating me, it has to go.

I know, it's easier said than done.

When I can't stop thinking about it, I imagine "throwing it away."

I imagine tossing it out into the universe, giving it over to that force that guides everything, and saying, "Here. You take it. I don't want it anymore."

Then I focus on what I need to do.

The problem comes back, but when it does, I throw it away all over again.

And I repeat, "Here. Take it. I've had enough."

I keep doing it until it doesn't come back.

Eventually, it stops or takes care of itself.

In the meanwhile, I take care of myself.

Like Tending a Garden

Reading daily encouragements and reflecting is like gardening.

When I look around my garden, I appreciate how nice everything looks, I think about how each plant is doing, decide whether I need to fertilize and which areas I need to weed.

It's the same thing with reading encouragements and reflecting.

I become grateful for all the things that I have, consider how various parts of my life are doing, decide where I need to put a little more effort and where I need to stop some negativity that's beginning to crop up.

Unlike gardening, it only takes a few minutes.

And when I think about it, why wouldn't I take those few minutes first thing in the morning?

I wouldn't go without eating, showering, getting dressed, brushing my teeth, or combing my hair.

So, why wouldn't I take care of the spiritual me too?

My Life is Becoming So Much Easier

As I was reflecting this morning, I realized how much easier my life has become.

I've become much less prone to extreme reactions and insisting on having my own way.

The temper tantrums rarely happen anymore.

It's unusual for me to walk off in a huff or sulk.

When I do feel resentful, it doesn't last for very long.

I feel a lot less selfish and self-centered.

I'm open to listening to what people have to say, accepting of their ideas, and forgiving them if I think they've done something wrong.

Even forgiving of myself.

Imagine that!

I'm feeling more gratitude and joy than I ever thought possible.

I'm not struggling.

Life has become as I always hoped it could be.

That's amazing.

When I Do Become Discouraged

Sometimes I feel discouraged or down when everything is going well, and I'm a bit surprised.

But I remind myself not to get down on myself because of it.

I remind myself that, overall, everything has been so much better than it used to be.

I stop and reflect on what I'm doing—what might be causing me to feel this way.

I might be doing too much or expecting too much.

It might be a good time for a breather.

Time to step back. Take a break. Recharge myself.

Time to let things percolate on their own.

Watch and see what needs to be done, if anything.

It might also be a good time to reevaluate my expectations.

Maybe lower them.

Or go in another direction, at least for the moment.

Take on something new that I might enjoy.

When I do these things, I usually feel better.

"That's silly" is Just Plain Silly

One thing that I keep working on when someone suggests something that they think might be helpful is my quick dismissal of it with "That's silly."

My brush-off of an idea before I fully consider it is one of the biggest blocks to learning something new.

Even if I don't think the idea is a good one, I can still test it to see if it works.

Sometimes even if an idea doesn't work well, parts of it may be workable and better than the way it's being done now.

Sometimes, too, it can lead me to consider other ideas that I hadn't considered before as a result of this new one.

I have nothing to lose when I listen—other than remaining where I am, maybe ignorant, maybe unhappy, maybe wondering why things aren't getting better, and wondering what I'm doing wrong.

Everybody Can Help Someone Else

I once heard a story about a homeless person, we'll call him Joe, who walked around a particular neighborhood every day.

As with most homeless people, Joe's clothes were old and torn, and he kept his possessions in a broken-down shopping cart.

As the story goes, one of the neighbors gave Joe new clothes to wear. And Joe thanked him for his kindness.

However, Joe was soon wearing his same old clothes, and the neighbor asked him, *What happened to the clothes I gave you?*

I was told that Joe smiled and said that he donated the clothes to a nearby shelter for people who *really* needed them.

He thanked my neighbor and said that the shelter greatly appreciated the donation.

The point is, everybody can help someone else.

Joe did.

How to Autocorrect Effectively

I find that trying something new is like relying on autocorrect while texting.

There's bound to be a bunch of mistakes, or in this case typos.

So, I try hard to remember to check my texts before I send them.

It's the same with new things. I'm going to make mistakes.

So, I try to check for them before I finish.

I find that when I do send a text with typos, chances are most people will still understand it.

If they don't, they usually text me back asking for clarification.

The same thing happens with something new.

People will be able to understand it, but if not, they'll ask for clarification.

I don't sweat the mistakes I make today when doing something new.

It's a learning experience.

Besides, like texting, we autocorrect as we go along.

On Stubbing My Toe

My father said that if I moved too fast, I'd probably end up stubbing my toe.

There's a good deal of truth to that expression.

However, I thought my father was admonishing me for being impulsive.

Plus, it made me worry that I would stub my toe—and for me that meant I failed in some way.

Today, I see that expression more realistically.

He wasn't telling me that I was impulsive.

He was telling me that there would always be bumps in the road, and if I didn't take it easy, I wouldn't see them.

So, it would make sense to go slow.

But I also realize that sometimes I stub my toe whether I'm moving fast, slow, or just doing something that I do every day.

And it doesn't mean failure.

Toe stubbing just happens, occasionally, with daily living.

Tongue Slipping

I once had a poster that read, "Oh Lord, let my words be sweet because tomorrow I might have to eat them."

It always made me smile and think about what I wanted to say and how best to say it.

Recently I read a similar expression, "It's better to slip on your feet than on your tongue."

That too made me smile.

I've learned that when I fall, I can get up, dust myself off and start again.

But I may not be able to take back my words.

Sometimes they hurt others too much.

So, I try to keep my thoughts and emotions on a positive plane—encouraging myself and others as best I can.

If I do slip, I apologize as quickly as possible.

Though I prefer not to eat my words at all, if I can help it.

Tap the Cane

I was reflecting this morning, imagining what it's like for someone who is blind to use a cane in order to feel what's ahead of them, so that they can move forward safely without hitting obstacles in their way.

I feel like I'm learning to do that in my own life.

I'm learning how important it is for me to "feel" my way around first, before I move forward.

I'm learning that a little caution is good for me.

I'm realizing that when I rush into things, I don't "see" obstacles that are in my way.

But a little "tapping of the cane" can help me to feel safe moving forward—not rushing into things "blindly."

Learning from Your Mistakes, Not Mine

There is an old proverb that I like, "A wise man learns from other people's mistakes while a fool learns only from his own."

I remind myself how important it is to learn from other people.

To watch what works and what doesn't.

To keep an open mind about what people do and think rather than dismissing things right away.

Relying only on my own thinking is like "going to court and being my own attorney."

What do I know about the law, when I could have someone represent me who does it every day for a living?

Relying on my own thinking is like "wandering around in an unknown neighborhood."

That can be dangerous.

So, I'm learning to listen to other people's experiences and borrow their road maps to get around.

I like getting all the help I can get.

That's a nice change for me.

It's Easy to Criticize, More Difficult to Correct

It only takes a few moments to point out somebody else's mistakes.

But it takes a heck of a lot longer to undo the damage when I do that.

I overlook how much time, effort, financial and emotional investments that someone may put into a particular pursuit.

And I've forgotten how hurt I become when someone does that to me.

I'm learning to go slowly, and if I say anything—to be sure that my remarks are constructive and only about the activity, not the person.

My remarks need to be well-thought-out and positive, not a knee-jerk or negative reaction.

I also have to be ready to offer my help—and if asked, be willing to get involved.

Otherwise, I need to stay quiet or just commiserate and express support.

I want to make things better, not hurt someone in the process.

Recognizing their efforts means a lot.

Every Maybe Has a Maybe Not

I laughed when I recently read that *every maybe has a maybe not*.

I thought, What the heck does that mean?

But as I reflected on it, I realized that the expression meant that everything that might happen, might also not happen.

Although I plan and hope for something good to occur, it could turn out otherwise.

My intentions may be good, but my words might not reflect what I feel.

Or they may be misinterpreted.

Yesterday I was clear about what I wanted to do, today it may not feel right at all.

I have to remember that situations and people change, and things happen as they will.

I can try to control how I intend to act, what I plan on doing, and my possible reactions.

But I can't control everything.

I have to be ready to accept that *every maybe may also be a maybe not*.

The Importance of Routine Checkups

I read encouragements and reflect throughout the day.

My few minutes in the morning usually isn't enough to keep my mind clear all day long.

So, when I'm tired or uncomfortable, I stop and do a "routine checkup" to get myself back "on track."

I ask myself what I'm thinking about, and if I'm trying to be helpful and reasonable?

Have I reached my limit? Do I need to do something else?

I don't want my thinking to become muddled because I didn't take a few moments to recharge and maintain realistic perspectives.

Routine checkups keep me in a fit mental and emotional state.

I stop, rest, read and reflect.

I make the adjustments I need in order to keep a clear mind, to feel refreshed and ready to handle whatever I need.

Routine checkups make my day much more productive and enjoyable.

Those Nightly Checkups

My life is improving as I don't limit my daily encouragements and reflections to the mornings.

Or even throughout the day.

I also spend time reflecting before I go to sleep.

I ask myself:

Did today go according to plan?

If it did, I allow myself to feel good about it and the effort I put into it.

If certain things went wrong, I ask myself what can I change?

If there were moments that I was not as supportive as I might have been, how can I make up for it tomorrow?

If I was helpful to others, I allow myself to feel good about that too.

My checkup has to be balanced.

I spent too much of my life being self-critical.

I need to recognize when I'm doing well and what I'm doing well.

I get a good night's sleep after that.

Treat the Whole Day as an Opportunity

I was talking with someone about how I started off spending only my mornings reflecting and reading encouragements.

I told him how the time I spent doing this was fantastic.

I was experiencing positive changes.

But then I began to recognize that there were times during the rest of the day that could sort of go downhill.

I told him that it occurred to me to treat the whole day as an opportunity to reflect and encourage myself.

As I practiced this, my day remained very gratifying.

So, I said, since then I've added routine checkups throughout the day and even a nightly review.

I told him how helpful it's become.

My days now—by and large—only go uphill.

It's Not Always the Big Things That Mess Me Up

Sometimes I spend too much time worrying over "the big things," and it's the little things that trip me up.

I usually see the wall in front of me and decide ahead of time whether to slow down, turn around, go around it, or try to knock it over.

But I have to laugh.

It's usually the rock in the road that causes me to stumble, the fog that rolls in to block my view, or the distraction to the side of me that stops me from seeing that wall.

So, all in all, I have to watch the road ahead, while I still stay focused on what's immediately below me, around me, and what I'm feeling inside of me.

And then still—not take it all too seriously.

Something may mess me up anyways.

Listening to Angry People

A hard thing that I've had to learn to do is to listen to someone who's angry without getting angry back at them.

Most of the time when people are angry, they feel that way for a good reason, and it's probably worthwhile listening to what they have to say.

Though I may not always be able to handle it at the time, later when things cool down, I've learned to ask the person if they would be willing to go over what they were trying to say now that they're not so upset.

When I've gotten angry it's usually because I think that something should have been done differently or better.

So, it's worth the effort to listen to somebody else.

I find the same is true with quiet introverted people.

They have their story to tell too, and I can learn a lot from them.

The World Will Wait

It's good to pay attention to and keep up with world news.

It's not good when I let it affect me negatively.

I like to keep current, I like to have an opinion—but I don't like when I engage in arguments and hot debates.

This only saps my good energy.

The world will go on fine without me getting involved that way.

I can do my part in more positive ways to make it better.

I can vote, recycle, write letters to my congressman, attend rallies, donate to causes, and more.

These things can make me feel good about contributing to a better world.

But I have to stay within the limits of what I can handle emotionally.

My first responsibility is always to take care of myself and the people closest to me.

The rest of the world will have to wait.

I'm Independent

I like to do what I want, when I want, and how I want.

I think for myself, and no one, not even you, can tell me what to do.

I told this to a close friend recently, who said in response:

> So, go ahead. Hit that wall, fall off that cliff, insist you're right when everyone else says you're wrong. Go your own way, knock yourself out, and maybe wind up saying some foxhole prayer like, *God, get me out of this one last time. Please!*

I looked at him and shook my head.

Okay, I get it! I said. *You're right. I can be very obstinate in my insistence on how independent I want to be.*

I'm much more independent now by relying on daily reflections and encouragements than I ever was by blindly insisting on not needing any help at all.

It's a nice paradox.

When It's Them, Not You

I'm learning that if someone criticizes me, I have a choice.

I can ask them, *What might be better?* Or, I can walk away.

If someone is laughing at me, I have a choice.

I can ask them, *What's so funny?* Or, I can also walk away.

If their criticism is helpful, I thank them and learn from it.

If what they're laughing at is funny, I laugh too.

But if someone is mean-spirited, I say, *That's rude.* And I walk away.

I'm learning not to take others' remarks or actions to heart.

People act this way because of their own fears and insecurities.

Not much different than how I act at times.

So, I try to be forgiving as I would hope they would be with me.

If there is something to be learned, great.

I can make changes.

If not, I move on.

Focus Can Be a Funny Thing

When I think about all the things that I have focused on, I have to laugh.

I've reflected on moving too quickly and stumbling on something small, being distracted by something small and running into a wall, or focusing on too many things and missing everything.

So, what's a person to do?

I suppose I should lighten up. Not take myself so seriously.

I'm going to stumble on things and trip—for sure!

When I don't look around me, I'm not going to enjoy the view.

And when I am enjoying the view, I'll probably make a wrong turn and end up someplace else.

Is there no winning?

Nah.

But maybe if I focus on what I need to focus on, I'll focus on whatever corrections I need to focus on as I go along.

How's that for a clear focus?

Ha.

So, What's My Choice for Today?

So, what's my choice today?

Am I going to make the time this morning to read encouragements and reflect?

Or am I so busy, so happy, and doing so fine on my own that I don't need any help right then?

I'll do it later.

Of course, later may be too late.

Things can start to get out of hand quickly, I can become discouraged, demanding to know what happened and why things aren't working out the way I want them to.

That sense of peacefulness that I like to have is just around the corner.

But I don't always take the time.

So, I have to ask myself, what's my choice today?

Am I willing to stop, reflect and gain that sense of peace this morning?

Or will I be too busy—winding up demanding and feeling that everything is going wrong?

My choice.

Sure, Why Not Make It Worse?

Nothing is so bad that a little more anger won't make it worse.

Do I add to the fire?

Do I enjoy tossing more wood onto the flames?

Or, do I pour water on it, helping to put it out?

Do I allow the fire to smolder while I continue to enjoy the heat?

Or, do I throw dirt on it, attempting to put it out completely?

How I deal with conflict is up to me.

I can make things worse, let things smolder or I can settle things down.

What's my choice for today?

Time for a checkup?

Is there something bothering me today?

If there is, have I taken time to reflect on it?

What's it about?

Is it because of what someone said or did?

Have I told that person how I feel?

Do I know what's bothering me? What I'd like?

Am I making things worse?

Am I being mean-spirited? Sour grapes?

When I do a checkup, I look at my part in the situation.

It's usually not the other person's fault entirely.

Nor is the other person so powerful that I have to become their victim.

So, I look within myself for answers, find my own power, and try to use it wisely.

I fix things when I can, rather than tear things down or let them build up inside of me.

If they can't be fixed, I move on.

Staying in the Middle

Today I try not to go to extremes.

Life's greatest pleasures seem to occur by staying in the middle.

Just being a friend among friends.

A member of the family.

A solid employee, not necessarily the best but certainly not the worst.

And as I take part in different groups and community activities, I'm finding great comfort in just belonging.

I'm not striving to be better than anybody, critical of anyone, or changing anything.

Ha. Neither am I staying at the edges, last seat in the room, closest to the door, arriving late and leaving early, or worrying about being accepted or not.

I'm enjoying being there along with everyone else.

All I want to do is be in the middle—feeling like I'm a part of things.

Like I belong.

The *Why Me's?*

If I'm regularly asking myself *why me*, it's time to look at the *probably's*.

Like, I'm *probably* trying to make everything go my way. The way I want them to be.

And it's *probably* time to lighten up on my expectations and accept life as it's happening.

It's also *probably* time to take the focus off of me and put the focus on the people around me, asking them if they need anything and if I can be of help.

And *probably* as I find myself thinking about others and do something helpful for them, I'll feel useful and good about myself.

That seems to be a real effective cure for the self-pity of the *why me's?*

The *Just a Little More* Syndrome

There are days when I suffer from what I call the *Just a Little More* syndrome.

If only I had *just a little more*. Not a lot. Just a little.

A little more of this or that. Come on, just let me have *just a little more*.

Some days though, whatever it is, when I get it, it's just not going to be enough.

And then there are those days when I feel life is asking me for *just a little more*.

I'm being asked to be just a little kinder, a little more patient, a little more forgiving, or a little more loving.

Not a lot, not really.

Some days *just a little more* can be too much to ask for and some days *just a little more* is something that anyone can do. Even me.

I just have to know the difference.

Outside and Inside

I love the feeling of the warmth of the sun on my face.

I go outside, turn my face to the sun, close my eyes, and feel that goodness radiating through me.

It's the same kind of feeling that I get when I practice daily reflection and reading encouragements.

I get that warm feeling radiating through me as I recognize how peaceful life can be and how much I feel that I'm part of it.

Outside and inside, I like that warmth.

I'm finding nothing good comes from staying in the dark, stubbornly standing my ground, or refusing to take part in things.

So, today, I turn my face towards the sun as well as facing my inner self, and try to feel the warmth that radiates from both.

Happiness vs. Stability

As time goes on, I know I'm becoming happier.

And I'm becoming happier as a result of my continuous practice of reading daily encouragements and reflecting.

But what's really happening is that I'm becoming clearer about what I want and how I'm relating to everybody and everything around me.

This clarity has led me to a more satisfying way of living, making transitions from one thing to another easier, and finding coping with surprises to be much less disruptive.

So, I'm happier.

But not everything turns out happy.

Stressful times happen, unpleasant or unfortunate events can occur, and we can also lose loved ones.

The daily discipline that I have developed is what keeps me going, helping me to grapple with and work through these losses and setbacks.

Happiness is nice but maintaining my stability and balance with regard to all things is most important.

Questioning the Universe: It's Not Fair

From time to time, I find myself torn apart by that eternal question: why do good things happen to bad people and bad things to good people?

It's not fair!

But as I reflect on it, uncomfortably, I know the sun comes up each day and shines on everyone and everything.

It does not discriminate.

So, for me, it's not that life is unfair as much as it just doesn't make distinctions among those who participate in it and everything that exists.

It may sound too philosophical but it's the only way I can make sense of it.

It's me who must discriminate, choosing between right and wrong, helpfulness or mean-spiritedness.

Yes, I feel helpless when bad things happen, and I want to scream, *It's not fair!*

But the power that I do have is within me—to love, to help, and to continue to do whatever I can.

Beginning Suggestions on Reflecting and Meditation

I wasn't sure how to meditate in the beginning.

So, I did some reading, and this is what I learned:

I find a comfortable sitting position, with my palms face up on my lap, and my back as straight as possible. I like to lean back against something.

I close my eyes or focus them on something in front of me.

I concentrate on my breathing, breathing in for 3-4 beats and out for 5-6 beats.

If I start thinking about something, as soon as I am aware that I'm thinking, I focus back on my breathing.

In the beginning, I only did this for a few minutes. That's all I could handle.

With practice, I settled down and relaxed.

And I didn't need to do it for long periods of time to get good results.

With practice, I got the hang of it.

I like meditating now.

Who Am I Really Lying To?

Sometimes I lie when I don't mean to.

I even want to twist that around by saying I don't *really* lie, I just have some temporary trouble admitting the truth.

LOL.

What that *really* means is that I'm having trouble accepting something about myself.

The question is: How long can I keep this up?

Eventually, I don't remember what I said, I get caught up in my words, I start to squirm and deny whatever it was that I said or didn't say.

It's not a fun way to live.

So, I'm trying my best to be honest, clean up whatever mess I might have created, and give myself some peace of mind.

That old saying applies, "The truth shall set you free."

I want to be free from twisting the truth, lying to you and to myself.

Being Supportive Rather Than Contradictory

While reflecting this morning, I imagined a conversation between two people.

The first one said, *What a beautiful day it is today!*

The second one replied, *You didn't think it was so beautiful yesterday!*

The first one, feeling criticized, shrank back, saying, *Well, that was yesterday.*

The moral?

Each day is its own day, and each person lives each day anew.

But this is also about how people communicate.

I don't need to make someone uncomfortable about what they said previously.

If I'm concerned about how someone was feeling before and how they're doing differently today, I can ask.

But I don't need to contradict them.

Everything changes, including me.

I don't want to make someone uncomfortable nor have someone make me uncomfortable by being rudely reminded of previous seemingly contradictory remarks or activities.

Now that's a mouthful, isn't it?

Making the World Better

I'm seeing as I reflect and read encouragements, how much good there is in the world.

Sure, there are a lot of bad things.

But there are as many, if not more, good things to be had and to be enjoyed.

I didn't always see it this way.

Now I try to see the good in people and in situations.

I'm not trying to be a Pollyanna. The world is far from perfect.

But so am I—and I spent too much of my time being negative.

It's important for me now to see the positives.

I enjoy telling people about what I see as being good in them and the world.

And I'm finding that they enjoy it too and feel uplifted as a result.

If you believe in blessings, and I think I'm beginning to, seeing the world in a positive light is an absolute blessing.

It's Let's Make Today "Real Simple" Day

Let's make today real simple.

I can either be content today or miserable.

I choose content.

So, like water off a duck's back, I'm going to let everything roll right off my back too—just for today.

Case closed.

Perspective is Everything

When I think about the world, how it began and continues, it is inconceivable to me.

I know science has studied it, mathematicians have created formulas to represent it, artists try to illustrate it, but no one can fully grasp the theory of everything.

I can only sit back in amazement, overwhelmed, stunned by how wondrous it is.

How did all this ever come to be?

Now, what does all this mean to me as I scarf down my breakfast, quickly get dressed, and rush out to sit in traffic?

I try to hold on to that feeling of not understanding how everything was created, hold on to that amazement and appreciation, that feeling of being stunned, as I go through this busy and sometimes frustrating day.

That perspective, for me, is the theory of everything.

Living is Like a Painter Painting

During a meditation, I was imagining how an artist paints his painting.

How he studies his subject.

How he puts his thumb up in the air to get a sense of perspective.

How he dabs his paintbrush into colors to get the right tones as well as the right texture.

And then, and only then, does he place a few strokes on the canvas.

The key here being: a few strokes.

I don't see him painting the entire painting all at once.

I imagine him taking his time, going slow, stepping back and studying, and then stepping forward and applying a few more strokes.

I consider how I might live my life from imagining how the painter paints his painting.

Slowly, studying, and applying only a few measured strokes at a time.

Rushing and Doing

Where does this urge to keep rushing and doing come from?

Rush. Rush. Rush. Do. Do. Do.

Sometimes I hate sitting still. Hate having time on my hands.

So, I rush and do things only to find that I want to continue rushing and doing even more.

It becomes addicting. I can never do enough.

Obviously, when that happens, I need to stop.

No one is looking over my shoulder, urging me on, making me do more.

Nor do I need to be looking over my own shoulder, criticizing myself for not doing enough.

So, I make myself take breaks.

I practice allowing myself to have some time on my hands.

I remind myself to be satisfied with what I've already done.

Even if I feel I could have done more.

I remind myself—there's always tomorrow!

Now's the time to rest. Enjoy!

Oh My, There's Always Tomorrow

Someone suggested an exercise to help me stop rushing and doing.

I was told not to finish whatever I was working on today.

Then, I should try to recognize how that made me feel.

It was suggested that I write my reactions down. Not dwell on them or berate myself.

Just recognize how I felt.

Then, tomorrow, I was to consider how the world did not end because I didn't finish.

If I felt anxious, I was to remind myself that it's only me making me feel that way.

Nobody had left me any messages saying that I was wrong for not finishing.

I was to feel satisfied with what I did complete.

Then, I might decide whether to work on it some more, complete it, or even work on something else instead.

It was my choice.

Because, oh my, there's always tomorrow to get something done.

Behind Every Opinion

I usually have an opinion because I don't like something and want it to change.

Or, because I do like something and I don't want it to change.

It all has to do with change: wanting it or not wanting it.

And behind that is: fear of change.

What am I really afraid of?

What is it that I fear losing, fear that I won't like if it happens, or fear that I can't continue to cope with?

How much control can I realistically exert over any of this?

How much will I upset myself and others by fighting change or refusing to accept what is?

And, is it worth it?

Or, is it best to accept that everything eventually changes and to adapt as best I can?

I will always have opinions, yet today I will try to remain as peaceful as possible within myself and the world.

If Letting Go Doesn't Suit You

Letting go is difficult.

Sometimes I take a different approach.

Rather than letting go, I wish for good things.

If I'm upset with someone, I focus on wishing good things for that person.

When I do that, then I don't spend time figuring out how to "let go" of my upset feelings.

I also find it comforting to wish someone well.

But I have to be careful because my "sarcastic side" could slip in some unwell wishes—wishes that would benefit me rather than them.

For example, wishing someone gets a promotion outside of my department so I don't have to deal with them again. Ha.

But who knows?

It might fall back on me.

I might be the one getting the transfer away from that upsetting person but to someplace I don't want to go and without the promotion.

Be careful what I wish for.

Eating is a Little Like Living

I've been focusing again on my eating habits.

Aside from eating small, well-balanced, and healthy meals throughout the day, I've been paying attention to how I'm eating.

There are times when I scarf down my meals and concentrate on other things while I'm eating.

I'm not taking time to really enjoy my food.

So, I've been practicing taking smaller bites, chewing more slowly, and concentrating on tasting my food, appreciating the flavors and textures.

It's also making me want to choose foods that I clearly like to eat.

Eating is a lot like living.

I need to take both in small bites, savor what I'm doing without distractions, and decide whether the meal, like my life, is what I would like it to be.

Staying Open

Something simple struck me this morning.

If I keep an open mind, then I'll see things that I normally wouldn't.

And if I close my mind, nothing comes in at all.

I know. It's too simple and too obvious.

But what I'm trying to do is to pay attention to how I initially react to things as I go through the day.

I'm trying to notice if I am really keeping an open mind.

When someone says something to me, what's my reaction?

Do I think: *That's not right. That's stupid. I'm not going to do that.*

Is my mind truly open?

So, I stop and ask myself: *Could it be right? Is it really stupid? Can I try that?*

Then I ask that person to tell me more about what they're suggesting.

Who knows how good it might be—unless I close my mind completely.

Holding on Much Too Long

I don't know about you, but I like to hold on to things.

Many of those things are precious, like memories, picture albums, and gifts.

But there are some things that I hold on too much too long.

Like resentments and anger, guilty feelings and shame, worries and fear, to name a few.

These things eat away at me and deprive me of times that I can be enjoying myself and the people I care about.

Today, I'm going to do something about it.

I'm not going to hold on to things that are not good for me or for the people around me.

I will use my tools and focus on constructive thoughts and activities

I am not going to waste my time or anyone else's either.

Slow Down to Move Forward

If I take things slower, I can move around more easily.

I stumble less and I make fewer mistakes

By going slower, I'm much more able to appreciate what I'm doing which makes my day that much more pleasurable.

I feel less pressure to get things done right away and consequently, I take more breaks.

With more breaks, I have time to breathe and allow myself to be inspired.

And that's another thing—feeling inspired.

How great is that!

But it only seems to happen when I slow down, make the time to listen to other people as well as to my inner self.

When I'm rushing, there's no time for any of that.

Rushing Gets You Nowhere

Rushing gets you nowhere.

The irony of that line makes me laugh.

How many times do I rush to do things?

How often do I feel like I've got to get something done and over with now!

But all I get is myself crazy—and the people around me crazy too!

What am I doing when I act this way?

What am I really accomplishing?

Not much, really.

When I go slow, I enjoy what I'm doing and I generally get things right, or at least close to it.

When I'm rushing, I usually miss a lot of the important stuff as well as the good stuff.

I end up spinning my wheels a lot, and for what?

To go nowhere, really.

What I'm Trying to Achieve

There are days when I feel that reflecting and reading daily encouragements is a sacrifice.

It's taking up too much time, I don't feel like it, I'd rather be doing something else, and so on.

When I feel that way, I take a break.

It doesn't do me any good to allow those thoughts and feelings to build up in me.

I only get resentful.

It's like anything I do when it becomes too much—the best thing to do is to take a break.

Daily reflection and encouragements are meant to build up my patience and willingness, not strain them.

Why be hard on myself when I'm trying to achieve the opposite—to relax and take life as it happens?

So, I allow myself to feel what I'm feeling and take that break.

Because that is what I'm trying to achieve.

Humor, Comfort, and Trust

How I Start My Day

My father spent ten minutes every morning drinking coffee and chuckling over the newspaper comic strips.

What a good mood that put him in.

My mother would hum aloud while making breakfast for us kids and getting us off to school.

I was reflecting on how it doesn't take much to put us into good moods.

So, I focus on what puts me in a good mood, clearing away any bits of annoyance or disappointment from yesterday that might still be lingering.

I imagine myself starting off my day as if I was reading the comic strips or getting the kids off to school.

Or, in my case, spending a few minutes doing something that puts me at peace with myself and the world.

Like reading these encouragements and reflecting.

That's the way I like starting my day.

Have a Laugh Today

I've always enjoyed tongue slips.

They're like a mirror reflecting how I'm taking things too seriously.

For example, I've heard it said that if the facts don't fit the theory, change the facts.

I can't tell you how many times I've laughed out of frustration, throwing up my hands, wanting to change the facts.

Theodore Roosevelt purportedly said that if you kick the person in the pants who's most responsible for your troubles, you wouldn't be able to sit for a month.

Ouch.

But I have to smile. That's me!

I've come up with a few of my own, like:

> When I don't know what to do, I do what I know.
> And when I do know what not to do, I do that.
> But when I don't know when to do it, I do it whenever.

Then I think: Nobody gets this, which is why they don't understand.

Have Another Laugh

Here's another truth that makes me laugh, and it's so important to laugh. Especially at myself.

I can't and shouldn't take myself too seriously.

Mark Twain allegedly said: It ain't what you don't know that gets you into trouble. It's what you know for sure that just ain't so that does.

Boy, is that true.

It's those times when I insist that I'm right and I'm not, that gets me into trouble.

Sometimes I even make it worse for myself.

It's then that I not only insist that I'm right, but I rub people's noses in it.

Ouch, more trouble!

And later when I find out I'm wrong, the embarrassment is even worse.

On the other side of the coin, even what I do know that's right can get me into trouble.

That tree of knowledge is a real tricky thing. Ha.

Good Judgment

I'm coming to appreciate using judgment.

Up to this point, I've only considered using my judgment in respect to judging other people and judging them harshly.

I'm now understanding the word also means the ability to recognize right from wrong.

It's my judgment, and my use of good judgment, that keeps me safe.

It helps me to decide which of several paths might be the better one to take.

It's my judgment that guides me to self-correct when my initial judgment is a little off.

And I certainly don't want to use bad judgment.

Nor do I want to make snap judgments—ones that I make impulsively before I have all the facts.

And I definitely want to stop using such harsh judgment of other people as I have so many times in the past.

How's that for good judgment? Big smile.

Becoming Freer

As I continue to reflect and read encouragements, I find myself freer.

I am more accepting of my thoughts and feelings.

I am more accepting of people and situations.

I am more accepting of my reactions and less prone to impulsively act on them.

I am less constrained or weighed down by circumstances and events.

The world and all these things no longer have the same deep influences over me.

It sounds strange for me to say this but what I've discovered within me is greater than the world outside of me.

And I am free to enjoy life, appreciate it, and even impact it in some ways if I choose to, but now with compassion and understanding, being supportive of the people and the world around me.

What I have found within me cannot be taken from me.

How's that for freedom?

Continuity

I find it comforting to know that the words I read today are going to be similar to the words I read yesterday—and, most likely, similar to the words I will read again tomorrow.

I need the continuity.

It's the same continuity that I want to maintain spiritually within me—because life around me can be so discontinuous and disorderly.

I need the continuity because I need to remember.

I need to remember because it's only me who can maintain that continuity within me.

I don't ever want to lose what I have gained and worked so hard for.

So, each day I return to reading these same messages, these same types of messages, and remind myself of these same hopes and beliefs.

Like Eating, Showering, or Getting Dressed

Reading daily encouragements and reflecting has become an important part of my life.

It's like eating, showering, or getting dressed.

It's something I do every day and don't want to do without.

It provides me with a sense of calm and peace that I never imagined possible.

I know—because on those few days when I don't do it, I don't feel quite right.

I feel like something is missing.

But by taking that time each day, especially in the morning, I feel whole and complete.

Ready to deal with the day, I feel renewed and refreshed.

Why would I do without it, when it makes me feel so good?

After all, I wouldn't go without eating, showering, or getting dressed, would I?

It's Not a Matter of Sacrifice

I don't have to sacrifice anything in order to change—or to become happier.

It's not like I have to overwork myself or stress myself out.

I don't have to give up anything, except maybe being miserable.

All I have to do is to try to understand that, for the most part, everyone's trying to do the best they can.

Including me.

I need to remember that everybody's intentions are usually well-meaning and that I need to be compassionate and appreciative.

It becomes much easier when I can forgive myself and others, and not demand so much or become overly stern.

Nothing though needs to be sacrificed.

In fact, it was suggested to me that if I'm not enjoying life more as a result of what I'm doing, I can have my misery back at any time.

Think Big or Think Small

Sometimes I still beat myself up.

Especially when things don't go as I expect.

But it's all in my mind.

Nobody has as high expectations of me as I have of myself.

The point, though, is that I try.

But is trying good enough for me? No!

I still expect perfection and get disappointed in myself when I seem to fall short.

I still worry that people will notice and they, too, will express disappointment in me.

Today, I remind myself to keep my expectations realistic.

And if it doesn't work out as planned, who cares?

I tried. And if I want or need to, I can try again.

Not everything works out perfectly.

I can think big, but I can also expect small.

Or if I want, I can think small and be happy with big results.

On Having Complete Understanding

I can never have complete understanding.

I wish I could.

I wish I could completely understand you, every situation I find myself in, and even completely understand myself.

Ha.

Now, that's something—completely understanding myself.

The closest I come to understanding is when I take time to read encouragements and reflect.

Watching my thoughts and feelings, acknowledging them as they come and as they drift away, replaced by new thoughts and feelings passing through my mind.

It's a process of watching and acknowledging and watching some more.

That's not a bad way to understand things.

But even then, when I think I understand, there's usually more to it than meets the eye—or it changes from what I thought it was to something else.

Ironically, that's what I call complete understanding.

Knowing that everything changes or there's more to it than I think. And it's all a process.

On Having Humility

It's a good thing to be humble.

I understand it to mean accepting who and what I am reasonably and realistically—knowing my limitations and my abilities.

It was pointed out to me that there are geniuses, great achievers, who remain humble because they remember that their abilities are gifts they were born with.

As they accomplish remarkable results, they remember that they are no greater or better than anybody else.

We are all born with innate talents.

None of us are any less or more than anyone else.

As Popeye would say, "I am what I am."

In Hebrew, the unpronounceable name for God is YHWH which means "I am that which I am."

I try to remember that we are all that which we are.

We each possess our own talents, remaining grateful for what we have been given and remaining humble in our accomplishments.

Locking up the House

Every night I make sure that my house is locked up tight.

I check that the windows are shut and latched, the lights are off, and the outside doors are secured.

It was suggested that every night, before I go to bed, I do the same with my fears and worries.

Lock them out and get a good night's rest.

Because at night, in the dark, my mind would be too muddled to work on any problems.

The worries become exaggerated—being replayed over and over again.

Instead, I focus on being grateful for another day, knowing that I have the ability to make whatever changes are needed in the morning, and locking my house up tight for tonight.

After a good night's rest, in the light of day, after reading encouragements and reflecting, I am then ready to face everything with a clear mind and renewed courage.

No Excuses

There are times when I don't feel like reading encouragements and reflecting.

I have to force myself to do it.

I find myself coming up with excuses.

But, in my heart, I know they're just that—excuses.

I'm like the little kid who is whining, "I don't wanna!"

But I know that when I get down to it and spend those few moments in quiet reflection, it will make a world of difference for me.

That whiney kid will leave, and I'll breathe a lot easier.

And I'll be happy that I did not allow my excuses to take me away from something that I enjoy and need so much.

I can't always let that little kid in me have his own way.

Those Silly Fears

When I stop rushing, where will I be?

If I stop being angry and nothing changes, what happens then?

What will I worry about if I'm no longer worried? Ha!

If I give up being jealous, will I appreciate what I do have?

Am I capable of having peace and understanding?

Practicing patience and compassion?

How about kindness, good judgment, and forgiveness—will I have those too?

Will I be able to set reasonable limits?

Will my fears come back from time to time?

Of course.

I'm human, not perfect.

It's all a process to keep working on.

What Does Me Good?

Admitting that for the past couple of days I have not been practicing daily reflection and encouragement does me no harm.

But it's not doing me any good either.

Strong Roots

Reading daily encouragements and reflecting helps me grow spiritually.

It was suggested to me that it's similar to how a plant grows.

A seed is planted in good soil and then needs regular watering and sunlight.

With that, it begins to grow roots and a stem.

As the stem grows higher, the roots spread and grow deeper to support it.

I feel like I'm doing the same things.

Through daily reflection and reading encouragements, I am planting myself in good soil and providing myself with the light, water, and the space that I need in order to grow.

I'm developing a firm stem and good strong roots to support myself with.

So, each morning I stop, smile, and reflect, asking myself, *how is my spiritual garden doing today?*

Do I have everything I need to continue to grow?

Running Spiritual Errands

At times when I'm reflecting, I think about someone and what I can do for that person that might be helpful.

It may mean just talking with the person, but at other times there may be some action I can take.

For example, someone might have told me about something they would like and I might decide to get it for them.

Or, that they were going on a trip and that I could offer to take them to the airport.

It could be as simple as giving someone flowers to cheer them up or helping them with something at work.

Trying to be helpful to people *makes me feel grateful*.

Like I'm running a "spiritual errand" by doing something positive for someone else.

I have to smile because it makes me wonder even more about other things I can do.

The possibilities seem endless. Ha!

Gratitude Revisited

Gratitude plays such an important part in my life.

So much so that I welcome being reminded to be grateful throughout the day.

It was suggested that I write a list of all the things that I am grateful for.

Then keep it handy at all times.

But, most importantly, to pull it out and read it throughout the day.

What a powerful tool!

It's hard to be upset when I acknowledge how much good exists in my life.

Put another way, there is so much more to be grateful for than to be upset about.

So, I pull out my gratitude list to remember—I also add new things to it as they come up.

But if I don't keep it close, I can't add to it or remember.

I need to remember that.

The Security of Seeing and Knowing

We are, obviously, not made with the ability to see or know everything.

For most people, that's just fine—they're content to just get through their day.

In fact, some prefer not to see or know things at all.

Makes life a lot easier as far as they're concerned.

For me though, just getting through the day was not enough.

And the "not knowing" made me anxious.

I wanted the "security of knowing" what was going to happen.

I wanted to control things.

Instead, now, by spending a few minutes each morning in reflection and encouragement, I get to see, feel, and understand the day ahead by envisioning differing perspectives and situations.

It's like having the ability to know and see things like I wanted to before but couldn't.

I like this "security of knowing" that comes from reflecting and thinking things through.

Something Very Powerful Happens

I don't know how or why it works when I make time each day to reflect and read encouragements.

But I know this: something very powerful happens when I do.

I become peaceful yet strengthened, happier through becoming more accepting, patient, and caring about people and problems, more open to suggestions and alternatives.

It really works.

And as I stop and reflect at various times throughout the day, these things become more intensified, and my day becomes even more productive and satisfying.

That's what I call powerful.

My Opinions Are Changing

My opinions are changing as I practice daily reflection and reading encouragements.

They are not as strong as they used to be and are much less likely to move me into immediate action.

I still have opinions.

I'm human.

But today I try to use them to my advantage rather than being moved by them to my disadvantage.

By reflecting on them—they lessen in intensity and my belief that I am always right.

I consider whether my judgment. and the action that it leads me to take, is a good thing.

Is it something that most people can benefit from? That is in most people's best interest?

And if I, or someone else, does something that turns out to be disadvantageous, I no longer have to sulk, run away, or get angry.

I can forgive them and myself.

And we can start again.

I Don't Miss My Old Ways

Because I make time every day to reflect and read encouragements, I feel much better.

I don't miss rushing to get ready in the mornings.

I don't miss getting upset with traffic and worrying about being late and everything I have to do.

I don't miss arguing at work and regretting it later.

At the end of the day, I don't miss feeling that I need to "take something" to release the tension.

I don't have to have a drink or a drug or stuff myself with food.

Or whatever.

My days are pretty even-keeled.

I take breaks, I relax, and try to let the answers come to me, rather than my forcing them.

When I do feel stressed, I talk to someone, listen to music, take deep breaths, and reflect.

I use my tools.

I don't miss my old ways, *at all*.

That Little Voice

I hear a little voice in my head today that I didn't always hear—if I did hear it, I didn't pay attention to it.

Now, especially when I'm angry or upset, I hear it loud and clear.

It says, *Wait, do you really want to do this?*

I stop immediately and reflect.

Maybe I heard that voice before, and maybe I ignored it.

After a while, I probably just blocked it out.

And because I no longer heard it, I made life miserable for everyone.

Today, I hear and adhere to that little voice.

The answer to the question of whether I really want to do something is usually a resounding, *No!*

And then I don't do it!

Because the answer is that, most likely, it was only going to get me into trouble.

Life's much easier now that I'm listening.

The Camel and the Rich Man

There is a phrase in the Bible that impressed me: It's easier for a camel to go through the eye of a needle than it is for a rich man to enter heaven.

I'm not a religious person, but that expression hit home.

I stubbornly held on to things that stopped me from "entering heaven."

I held on to harsh judgments of others and to my resentments rather than to forgive and feel free.

I held on tightly to a false sense of pride and superiority—like I was a wealthy and arrogant man.

But these things kept me from feeling happiness.

They kept me from entering "heaven"—at least here on earth.

I could see that camel going through the needle much faster than I could see myself changing.

And all I really wanted to do was change.

But I wasn't ready yet.

I had to become ready.

Why Them? Why Not Me?

I used to get envious of other people.

I'd think, *Why them? Why are they so special?*

But now I think, *I'm doing okay. So, why am I upset over somebody else's good fortune?*

Being bitter doesn't make me any happier.

Is it really important who is first or who gets what?

As long as I'm doing what I need to do, isn't that all that matters?

Tearing somebody else down doesn't build me up.

Doing what's right, though, does.

Imaginary Levitation

Someone once told me that he would imagine himself levitating above a situation that was upsetting him so that he could try to see the situation from a different perspective.

I asked him to give me an example.

He said he used this technique when he was getting irritated at being stuck behind a slow-moving car in traffic and unable to pass.

He imagined himself floating above the car and being able to look down and see inside of it.

He saw grandparents driving the car, having a good time, laughing with their grandchildren, and enjoying their outing.

Then he imagined himself returning into his own car and he calmed down, thinking how nice it was to not have honked his horn at them and to imagine what fun they were having.

I decided that the next time I was upset, I might try some imaginary levitation.

Make Time to Change

Every day I have to adapt to change.

I've come to understand this as one thing that is constant: change happens every day.

I can count on that.

Yet it's these changes that can make life so interesting.

But it also can make life very challenging, and I can complain about how much work it can cause.

Still, if every day was the same, I'd probably be bored and complain about that too.

Ha!

I guess I'm just capable of complaining about anything and everything.

As I read this, I think my problem is that I just like to complain.

Uh-oh.

Time to make another change.

A Great Peace

The time that I spend in reflection and reading encouragements in the morning, as well as throughout the day, is my own special place that I can go to and find a peacefulness within myself.

No matter how stressful the day may get, the few minutes that I spend in that place calms me down.

It's a treasure that I am so grateful for, and I've come to realize that it's something that cannot be taken from me.

It's become my strength.

What a paradox: by finding peace, I gain strength.

My Morning Chuckle

This morning I found myself reflecting on how I need to care more about the world around me.

How I need to be more kind and understanding—patient.

How I need to treat everybody and every situation as I would want to be treated myself.

Then I laughed.

I thought: I need to treat everybody and everything *better* than myself...

Because I don't always treat myself so well.

Maybe (ha) I need to start with me.

It's a Matter of We

When I go charging into a situation, I meet my greatest enemy: myself.

I use myself as a battering ram, pushing my way into situations to get what I want.

That old devil in me arises: *You* don't matter. Only what *I want* matters.

And how far did that get me?

Not very.

Usually, I look around and everybody's left the room.

I've pushed them away. *More like I battered them.*

I forget that it's a matter of we.

Not me vs. all of you.

It's we. Us.

What do we know, what do we want, what can we do together?

No Battering Rams Required Here.

On Hate and Genocide

It's difficult enough to handle differences of opinion.

But the most difficult are those expressing hatred and harm to other people.

Although I stay away from debating or arguing, trying to practice acceptance of differing opinions, this is one area that's important for me to say something about.

However, I try not to demean myself or others by getting angry or being insulting.

I try to keep my comments focused on my disapproval of the opinion, not the person.

I talk about how they are treating or want a particular group treated in ways that they would not want to be treated themselves.

I take the high road in the conversation and when it has gone as far as it can go, that's when I go.

It's important though, for me, not to hide my head in the sand.

To take a stand.

The Light Switch Trick

Sometimes I imagine, when I'm about to reflect, that I have a light inside my body, and I flick the switch on.

And with the light on, I search my thoughts and my heart for any fear, anxiety, or ill feelings that may be lingering there.

I pay attention to any flickering light; that tells me to be careful, there's a faulty circuit.

I spend a few moments trying to identify what might be wrong and what I might need to do.

When I'm comfortable with what I've found out, I flick the switch off.

I rest for a while, letting myself cool down, in the quiet, in the dark.

I don't need the light then because I feel content, and when I'm ready, I slowly open my eyes, take a deep breath, and let the daylight switch take over.

Enjoy the Whole Day Spiritually

There are all sorts of work: housework, homework, office work, yard work, and so on.

I think the most important work is spiritual work.

All the other work rests upon that or develops out of that.

If I don't take time to read encouragements and reflect, then all the other work I do is just a matter of rushing around trying to get things done rather than putting thought into it.

Spiritual work has become a source of relaxation and pleasure for me—which then makes all the other work that I do relaxing and pleasurable too.

The truth is, I really don't work much at anything anymore.

I just relax and try to enjoy the whole day spiritually.

Do I Really Have a Choice?

Some people like the idea that we have a choice.

We can choose to be happy and spiritually fit or we can choose to be unhappy, mean-spirited, and disillusioned with life.

If the idea of having a choice helps you, then I say, *Great*.

For me, there is no choice.

The thought of becoming unhappy again is unbearable.

I never want to go back to the way I was.

I am afraid that if the choice were left up to me, I would choose poorly.

So, I rely on the fact that there is no choice anymore.

The days of choosing are over! Gone.

Every day I remember how unhappy I was—there is no going back.

I keep moving forward, reading daily encouragements, reflecting, and using all of the tools available to me.

That works for me!

Help! I Need Someone to Help

I've had to ask myself, do I wait to see the good in someone before I offer help?

Do I wait to decide whether someone is worthy of my help?

Or, do I just see that somebody needs some help and offer it?

Today, the answer for me is that if somebody needs help, then I offer it if I can.

It doesn't matter right then whether the person is good or not, or worthy or not.

Most likely because the person was helped, he or she will be grateful—and when someone is grateful, they usually end up being "good" and will usually want to help somebody else in return.

The judgment of others plays little part in my decision to be helpful.

If that were the case, given the way I used to be, I might not have gotten much help myself from other people.

Stand Ready

Although I want to see the good in everyone and be ready to help, I also realize that I have to be on guard if someone or some situation becomes negative, hurtful, or destructive.

I've heard it said, and I like this expression: We need to live with our heads in the clouds but with our feet firmly planted on the ground.

I need to be lovingly realistic and realistically loving.

I need to do no harm, yet I need to not allow harm to happen.

To myself or to others.

I need to live and love, but also to be watchful.

On vs. Off

When I notice that I'm thinking about someone or something more than usual, I know I'm "off" somehow.

I'm usually feeling something too. Maybe annoyance, disappointment, or confusion.

It's then that I open up my "tool kit" and get to work.

I start to reflect on the thoughts floating around inside my head.

Once I get some ideas of what it might be, I consider what things that I can do to address what's going on for me.

But if nothing comes to mind right away, I turn my thoughts to other people or situations in which I can be helpful.

And then I get to work.

I do my best not to waste my energy obsessing or worrying about what I'm not ready or able to change.

I prefer to contribute and stay involved.

I prefer to be "on"—not "off."

A Kind of Thinking

I try not to think that I can't do a certain thing or will never get a certain thing.

Especially to the point that I get distracted or upset.

Today, I am more positive in my thinking.

I try to imagine what I want and what I can do to achieve it.

Not with the expectation that I will get exactly what I want, but in the hope that I will do the best I can, consider all the alternatives that are available, and enjoy what I'm doing along the way.

Today, I believe that all the things that I hope for will follow from that kind of thinking and that kind of action.

Then, I'm usually satisfied with what I do get, and it might even be better than what I had hoped for.

It's a nice way to be.

What's Your Plan?

Some people talk about a master plan that a higher power or deity has for them.

Some people call it fate or destiny.

That's fine for them, but I have trouble thinking that there is a prescribed plan that I'm supposed to adhere to.

If there is a plan, I tend to think of it as a spiritual plan, a way of living.

And that plan suggests that I do the best that I can, reflecting on the situations that I find myself in, and changing and adapting as needed as I go through each day.

That plan has me being helpful, caring, and considerate.

It has me actively participating in and with the world around me.

So, if there is an individualized plan, that's the one I can follow and believe in.

That works for me.

I'm Not Happy—Boo-hoo!

When I'm unhappy, I work slowly towards making the changes that might be needed.

The key for me is to "work slowly."

Rushing out and making sweeping changes isn't easily accepted or received favorably.

Conversely, things generally don't get better if I hide my head in the sand, hoping that things will get better.

Change takes time. And patience.

I hate hearing those words.

But they're true.

Most good and lasting changes happen by taking "baby steps."

Wanting what I want when I want it, the "His Majesty, the Baby" syndrome, doesn't work well.

My demanding behavior usually makes matters worse.

Everyone adjusts better, including me, when change happens slowly, and we all agree on the changes.

Baby steps seem to work best.

What? Me Worry?

Why do I worry so much about today's problems when I really won't remember them by next week?

My father always said that to me.

It's true.

He'd tell me to think back to last week and asked if I could recall all the problems that worried me then?

He said that I might remember a few, but how many did I remember from two weeks before that? Or the month before? Or from last year?

I had to admit that I didn't remember most of my problems.

Overall, they worked themselves out or I worked them out.

Or, they really weren't all that important.

So, today's problems will soon be forgotten—and tomorrow will have its own new set to deal with. Maybe.

So why worry?

I'm just going to chill. Everything will be fine.

Maybe.

Have You Noticed?

I've noticed that there is no need to get into heated theological discussions about God or religion, or what's right or wrong.

There is enough room for each of us to have our own set of beliefs.

I think most of us would agree that we simply want to try, each day, to improve ourselves, bolster our spirits, and use daily encouragements and reflections as best we can.

We'd like balance in our lives and to cope as successfully as possible with daily issues.

We'd hope to actively participate in life and with the people we care about, not withdrawing or overreacting.

We'd want, all of us, to enjoy good health.

And we would agree that all of us strive for inner peace, and to seek something greater than ourselves to help guide us along the way.

Have you noticed that too?

The Unexpected Photobomber

I was once in a new city taking a picture of a famous statue when a stranger in a car drove by with his window open, faced the camera, smiled, and yelled, "CHEESE."

He laughed as he drove off, and I laughed too.

We never know when life is going to hand us a spontaneous experience and laughter.

Today, I like leaving myself open to these chance encounters.

I even tend to smile and yell, CHEESE, myself, when I see someone taking a picture that I, too, find myself in unexpectedly.

The "Do's" and "Try's" of Handling Problems

I do take lots of breaks.

I do distract myself with other things.

I try not to run away from life's problems.

I try not to throw up my hands and quit.

I do let my mind wander hoping new ideas will cross my mind.

I do ask other people for help.

I try to rest and maybe get back to a frustrating problem later.

I try not to slam into a complication head-on.

That only gives me a headache. Ha.

I try to put things into a proper perspective, and I do laugh about it.

And as I've heard it said oftentimes:

> When I do find myself in a hole, I try to stop digging.

Principles Vs. Flexibility

John Adams, Second US President, is quoted as saying, "Always stand on principle even if you stand alone."

It may be a great saying for him, but it's not for me. Ha!

Too many times when I've stood on my principles, I've stood there alone.

My stubborn insistence on being right has pushed many people away, leaving me lonely and feeling isolated.

Everett Dirksen, Illinois Senator, is credited with saying that the most important principle of all principles is to be flexible.

Andrew Carnegie, millionaire philanthropist, is thought to have said that all principles can be compromised to serve something greater.

My something greater is this: my ability to get along with others, to enjoy life, and to be productive.

So, I say:

> I try to have as many principles as possible
> because if the ones I'm using now aren't working
> I can try using a few others that might.

Laughter is Not Just Fun. It's Levitating.

When I need a rise, I try writing humorous lines of my own to help me not take things so seriously.

Things like:

- Most of my worries are just pigments of my imagination.
- If I think too fast, I get comprehended by the thought police.
- I try not to think less of myself. It's self-defecating. Ooh. Nasty.
- I try not to fool myself because I'm not sure if I'd know the truth.
- I think a cappella. But it gets lonely.
- I find everything works out when I let it.
- I do what I always do every time, only differently.
- When I think, "The hell with it," is when it usually works out best.
- Do no harm. Stop thinking.

Try writing a few of your own if you can.

It's always fun to play, "Let's Not Take Life So Seriously Now."

Add a Little Music

When I'm stressed and nothing else seems to be working, one of the tools that I have in my toolbox that calms me down and helps me get centered again is: music.

So, I crank it up.

I'll listen to my favorite songs and start singing along—that is, if you can call it singing.

But I don't care because music takes away *all* my immediate distress.

And don't tell anybody but I'll do some dancing too.

All the sound and movement really gets my energy up and running.

I'm told that dancing, like exercise, releases those "good" endorphins and lessens feelings of anger, anxiety, and depression.

If you haven't considered it, add some music to your life.

Become a song-and-dance man or woman.

On Trying Something New

I have my limits.

I didn't always know them.

I've learned not to go beyond what I'm comfortable with.

But now that I've learned about my limits, I remind myself that it's good to try something new, learn something different or take on a challenge.

Otherwise, life can get a little dull, even boring.

So, on occasion, I step out of my comfort zone, telling myself that if it gets to be too much, I can dial it back or stop.

I used to think that once I committed to something I had to remain committed to it even though it was making me miserable.

Today I've learned that I can stop when I've had enough, when it's time to move on.

Although I don't always like to leave my comfort zone, new things can be worth a try—but I won't know unless I try them.

The Truth and Nothing But the Truth

Even though I read daily encouragements and practice reflecting, little things still go wrong and big things still happen that throw me off course.

I get upset. I get anxious. I get teary-eyed. I get hurt. I get angry.

But today I know it won't last.

My emotional reactions to events are not as intense as they once were, nor do they stay with me as long as they used to.

Today, I know that situations change, and I will adapt with them as I go along.

Deep inside of me, I feel and I know, based on experience now, that everything is okay even if it seems upsetting to me today and I'm not sure yet about tomorrow.

It will work out and I will get through this.

That's the truth, and nothing but the truth.

Self-assessment

An important part of what I do is self-assessment.

So, I ask myself:

Did I do enough today? Could I have done more?

Am I satisfied with what I have accomplished?

Is there something I still need to finish?

Did I withhold anything? If I did, why?

Did I take enough breaks?

Did I ask for help? If I didn't, why not?

Do I need to stop what I'm doing? Move ahead, but differently? Have I reached my limits?

It's often good for me to write down the answers, so I can have a clear idea of what they are.

Answering them in my head is often not enough.

What I'm trying to do is to find balance, reasonableness, and some ideas about realistic ways to proceed.

Then I let it go, remembering that there's always tomorrow to finish things up.

A Natural Flow

There are days when my life seems to flow naturally.

I like it when it gets that way.

No bumps, no ups and downs.

It feels even-keeled and satisfying.

To be poetic for a moment, it reminds me of nature: like the changing of the seasons, one after the other.

Winter into spring, summer into fall.

Or, like night giving way to sunrise and then back to dusk.

I rest, awaken, reflect, and create.

My life now often moves along comfortably like these natural patterns and rhythms.

I'm finding my own pace and peace.

Things seem to flow—naturally.

How nice.

A Plan I Can Follow

I've spoken about this before.

When religious people tell me that there is a master plan that I need to adhere to, I start to smile because I immediately want to ask:

Can I see the plan?

Can I change the plan if it's not working for me? Is it negotiable?

I would probably appear too inquisitive and maybe somewhat meddlesome.

Most folks would probably tell me to simply relax and know that there is a plan for me.

But I'm not built that way.

I have enough anxiety already living with uncertainties.

It's an oxymoron for me to have to follow an invisible plan.

It's hard enough spending time each day just looking into my heart to see whether I'm comfortable with what I'm doing, hoping that I'm not harming myself or anybody else.

But—at least that's a plan that I can work with.

Regarding Professional Help

One thing I haven't discussed much is getting help from mental health professionals.

When I have a cough, I see a doctor. When I buy a house, I hire an attorney.

When I'm having severe emotional stress, like depression or anxiety, and it's interfering with my ability to function, I get professional help.

We've all needed help at one time or another.

It's no shame—we don't have to do this by ourselves.

And we shouldn't.

We seek help with other things, so for mental health and addiction issues, we get help from psychiatrists, psychologists, social workers, and others. There are numerous treatment and 12-Step programs available. At work, there is usually an Employee Assistance Program that is confidential and can help.

When things get overwhelming, I need all the help I can get.

And it's a real relief to get that help.

It's that simple.

No excuses, really.

On Being Loyal

I read once that when I'm feeling inadequate, I'm being disloyal to myself.

When I feel that way, I'm also being disloyal to the people around me who trust me.

The idea that I might be disloyal to myself and others is unsettling.

It's become important for me to believe and know that I'm capable of handling day-to-day issues and to be able to stand by the people I care about, to be helpful and consistent.

I cherish my sense of direction and purpose today.

I don't ever want fear to cause me, and the people I care about, to feel let down because I didn't trust myself, or to get help, with some new undertaking.

I don't ever want to be disloyal.

I've worked too hard and have come too far to let that happen.

This Really Works

As time goes on, and I continue to get the help I need, I realize how much my emotions and my reactions to life have leveled off.

I am much less prone to anger, hurt, fear, depression, or impatience.

I tend now *not* to react in ways that are *not* in my best interest, such as overeating or isolating.

I am much less disappointed with my life.

I have so many more days of enjoyment, helpfulness, and hopefulness.

I take care of myself now, and I do things that will benefit myself and others.

Today, I am grateful for everything I have.

I give thought to my life now, striving to be useful and wanting to participate in constructive ways with the people around me.

Life is so much better.

Is it perfect? No.

But this is really working.

A Deep Inner Calm

If I only had one wish, if I could only guarantee one result from practicing daily reflections and reading encouragements, if I could cultivate only one thing within me, it would be to possess a feeling of deep inner calm.

I try though not to think of it as something unachievable.

I try to have that feeling within me every day and throughout the day.

I have it when I think about everything I'm grateful for.

I have it when I take breaks throughout the day and refresh myself as much as possible.

I have it as I take deep breaths.

I have it when I laugh and when I compliment others as I go along.

I have it when I think to myself that I'm doing just fine and enjoying myself with others.

It's remarkable what these actions do for me—to achieve that one wish.

It works.

Sometimes I Read This Several Times Over

This can be another day filled with joy, discovery, and giving.

But if I wake up with a feeling of, *oh my goodness, it's morning already,* then it's not just another day for me.

It means that I'm already feeling worried and tense.

I quickly remind myself that I can get through this.

This heaviness won't last all day.

So, I have my coffee, eat my breakfast, read some encouragements, and reflect a little.

If I'm still feeling unsettled, I make the decision that all I have to do is get through this morning.

That's it. Nothing else. That's my job for now. I can handle that.

I think, *Whatever has me upset will take care of itself.*

There's nothing to rush about. Just take my time. It'll all be okay.

Sometimes I read this several times over if I need to.

What Was I Thinking?

When I'm having problems, it's mostly due to wanting *only what I want* and my reactions to *not getting my way*.

Well, maybe not mostly.

But a good deal of my problems are due to that.

But then again, maybe not a good deal.

Maybe just some small portion of my problems are caused by that.

But I've noticed that you're not too bothered by them as you simply keep telling me, *No*.

So, as I think about it, they're really not problems for me either—now that I've stopped thinking about me and only what I want and what I'm not getting.

What was I thinking?

Heavenly

Reading encouragements and daily reflection may not get me into heaven, that is, if I believe there is such a thing as heaven.

But it certainly has made my life heavenly.

And, it has definitely prevented much of the hell that I used to go through.

Someone once told me that if I wasn't happy with how I was doing today, I could get my former misery refunded by stopping what I was doing.

No need for a refund here.

I'm not stopping any time soon.

I'm very satisfied.

It's heavenly now.

What's a Higher Power?

I find it hard to imagine God.

I often wonder what He looks like, why I can't see Him or hear Him.

People have said things to me like, "God would overwhelm us if we could see Him," "You just have to have faith," or "God talks to us through other people."

While I understand the good intentions of people, these suggestions have not quite satisfied me.

Someone suggested that I develop my own concept of God.

I found that difficult too.

I've become most comfortable with the idea that yet another person suggested—that I hold on to an idea of God as I can't imagine God.

That worked for me.

I have no pretensions about my being able to imagine God.

It is beyond my abilities.

But I can live with the concept: God as I can't imagine Him.

That Higher Power, Continued

I cannot imagine a corporeal being overseeing everything—that vision of an older, wise person, male or female, pulling all the right levers and running the show.

However, I can feel a Divine Presence, a principle or set of principles that operate throughout the universe and over time.

A rhythm that does not change, like the seasons, constant and ever-present.

It is this rhythm, this presence, this principle or set of principles, that humbles me, and I equate it as being God or a Higher Power.

This entity which exists, obviously far greater than me or any one of us, effectuated all things to come into existence and continue to be.

That is something that I can connect with, feel a part of, and comprehend because I see its existence each day as clearly as the sun coming up in the morning and setting again each night.

Those Little Things

When I stop whatever I'm doing, even for a moment, and look around me, I can often spot refreshing and even inspiration messages in the simplest of activities.

But I need to stop what I'm doing and look.

I miss these things when I'm overly involved in something, charging forward.

For example, how encouraging it is to observe the ant that's carrying something ten times its size.

Or, how funny it is to watch that dog chasing its own tail. Not that much different from how I act sometimes.

How heartening to see the youngster break out laughing after the shock of realizing that he or she has just slipped and fallen.

So, stopping for a moment and watching the world around me is worth the effort.

It's little things that we see ourselves reflected in that help us to reset, lighten up or gain insight.

Do I Really Want Help?

Today's message is a simple one.

Maybe not.

Help is always available if I stop and seek it.

The question I have to ask myself is: Do I really want help?

I have to answer that for myself every day—and I have to be honest with myself.

Sometimes, without my even realizing it, pride gets in my way.

So, I have to ask myself a second time: Do I really want help?

And then, I have to ask myself still another question: Am I'm willing to ask for it, accept it and use it when I do get it?

Lights on, Lights off

I once read a poetic description of stars as flickering on and off because they are broken.

I don't think they're broken.

I think that, like most things, they take a moment to rest before they light up again.

I thought another fitting description of stars is that they are like hearts, pulsing light into the night.

No matter what, it made me think of how we, you and I, are so much like both hearts and stars— pulsating, shining our light on and off.

We are at our best when we rest after being active for a time.

We go dark, rejuvenating ourselves, in order to light up, to beat once again.

So, I ask myself, how well am I doing by turning off and resting regularly, so I can successfully keep cycling back on to beat and shine throughout the day?

The Road Sign That Reads: *Consider*

While I was reflecting this morning, I found myself thinking about all those signs that we read along the road like: Slow Curve, Children Playing, or Dangerous Intersection.

Then I imagined a sign that simply read: *Consider*.

At first, I asked myself, what is it that I'm supposed to consider? Why consider?

But it occurred to me that I might consider how good my life is, what to do next and the best ways to do it.

It took on a meaning, too, that if my life wasn't going as well as I would like, I could consider how to improve it.

Then, smiling, I thought about watching for *Consider* signs all throughout my day.

I chuckled, considering how it could be one of the ways I could consider making my life considerately better.

Consider that!

It's a Group Effort

As I continue reading encouragements and reflecting, my outlook has broadened.

I recognize that when things were difficult for me—I affected a lot of people.

My immediate family, obviously.

But also my parents, employers, coworkers, and friends.

To some degree, relatives and even neighbors.

Many people were concerned and wanted to help, though I didn't realize it at the time.

I've since let them know that I'm sorry I worried them and how much I appreciate their desire to help.

I try now not to let things get that far out of hand and affect others as I did.

But I also realize that life is sort of a group "thing."

We're all concerned for each other, need each other's help, and are willing to help.

How wonderful that is.

I like to help too.

It really is a group effort.

The Repetition Compulsion

I've learned that there is a behavior pattern called a repetition compulsion.

It's when we do same the thing repeatedly, getting the same negative results, but expecting this time it will end differently, better.

Like the gambler who keeps losing but believes he'll win big the next time.

It's like me arguing and demanding that people agree with me even after they've said no.

Or, overextending myself, thinking this time I can handle it when I couldn't before.

Or, avoiding things thinking that by avoiding it'll go away, but it doesn't.

The scenarios are endless.

To break the cycle, though, *I have to admit to the behavior.*

Then, *I have to want to stop.*

Next, *I have to recognize* when I'm beginning to consider doing the behavior again.

As importantly, *I have to ask for help* to walk away. To not do it.

Before I start doing it again.

Here's the Choice

Here's the choice:

I can go through the rest of my day doing the same things I always do, in the same way I always do them, and doing them over and over again, getting the same unwanted negative results, and continue to make myself as miserable as I usually do.

Or, I can stop doing those same things, and make time each day to read encouragements, reflect, ask for help, and ultimately practice new behaviors that will most likely get the positive results that I'd like to have.

For example, I'd like to be hopeful, helpful, and peaceful.

So, what's my choice going to be today?

I'm Not Doing That Anymore!

There are certain behaviors in my life that I don't want to continue doing.

I know how they're going to end—and it's not wholesome.

Yet I can still feel compelled to do them, like I don't have a choice.

But that's not true.

In the past, I had to hit rock bottom before I could stop.

Today, I don't have to sink that low.

I can recognize these negative desires and patterns early.

A caution light blinks in my mind letting me know, *uh-oh, this isn't going to end well.*

An uncomfortable feeling sets in.

I pay attention to these warning signs, and I stop immediately and ask for help.

I talk about it with others, I get up and do something else, I get out my tool kit.

It's work, but it's a lot less work than what happens when I act in old self-defeating ways.

Don't Sweat the Small Stuff

I love that expression today.

I could obsess over the littlest things.

I could trip over my own feet and ruin my day—sometimes the whole week!

Instead of laughing at myself or at the really big things that are fully out of my control, I ruin my day obsessing over the littlest ones.

Well, nothing goes perfectly.

So, having said that, ironically, the expression *Don't Sweat the Small Stuff* works *perfectly* for me.

Ha!

When I say it, it makes me think of my feet and tripping myself.

I can laugh at that image now, I couldn't before.

I took myself, and everything, too seriously.

But now: Watch out floor, here I come!

LOL.

Down with Perfection

I can get down on myself when I think I didn't do as well as I thought I should have—that I wasn't perfect.

The question I ask myself now is: *Whatever happened to good enough?*

Whatever happened to: *I did the best I could, I enjoyed myself, or my heart was in the right place?*

Not everything is neat, tidy, and perfect.

Not everything gets wrapped up in pretty packages with no loose ends.

I now believe that being well-meaning, trying, helping, and caring are the things that matter most.

Expecting to be perfect is an imperfect expectation. Ha!

I say: *Down with perfect expectations!*

Today, I can live with loose ends and imperfect wrappings.

What I Try Not to Think About

I try not to think that I cannot do a certain thing—or that I will never get a certain thing.

Especially to the point where I get myself upset about it, and now it's a distraction.

Instead, I imagine what I'd like, decide what I can do to try to achieve it, and take the initial steps.

Not with the expectation that I'll get exactly what I want, but in the hope that I will, at least, enjoy working towards the goal.

I've found that good things usually follow from this kind of thought and action.

Then, because I am open-minded about alternatives, I can be surprised by what I do get, and it might be even better than what I hoped for.

The point is to not hold on tightly to what I think I want and to enjoy myself along the way.

All Kinds of Help

I have to laugh.

There are all kinds of help available these days.

Help which I call the *you're-on-your-own* kinds of help, such as *self-help*, *do-it-yourself-help*, and *I'd-rather-go-it-alone-all-by-myself-help*.

What I think I'm doing is *getting-all-the-help-I-can-get-help*.

I'm looking for both inner and outer forms of help.

I'm also doing the *we're-all-in-this-together-help*.

So, you can try all the *you're-on-your-own* kinds of help and good luck to you.

But me?

I can't do it on my own.

I need the other two.

Spilt Milk

If I make a mistake, if something goes wrong, I now say—so what!

Everybody makes mistakes.

I used to feel that I was the only one that could make a mistake and everybody would see it.

That's just not true!

I've had to get rid of that thinking, and I have no idea where it came from.

Today, I let myself feel bad for a moment if I make a mistake, because that's normal.

Then I think about how to correct it.

If I can correct it, I do it, and I feel good about it.

If I can't, *oh well,* and I move on.

No use crying over spilt milk.

I simply clean up the mess, pour another glass, and maybe even get some cookies to go along with the milk.

I'm grateful now that I can do that.

That Thing That I Seek

I can't talk about this enough.

As I read daily encouragements and reflect, I find myself connecting with something greater than just the immediate changes I'm trying to make.

Don't get me wrong,

I need to make all these changes.

But as I clear away all the past debris, I'm realizing that there is something beyond what I'm doing that is bringing me even greater joy.

I've described it before as something eternal or unchanging.

We don't all agree on what it is, but that doesn't really matter.

I think we all sense that something does exist which makes us feel at peace with the world and ourselves.

So, I keep reading encouragements and reflecting, trying to "tune in" each day to that entity.

To feel that sense of purpose, joy, and connectedness with the world.

It's that thing that I seek.

The Happiness Activity

I know now that I cannot be happy without some activity.

It may sound simplistic but happiness comes as a result of my doing something that makes me, as well as the people around me, happy.

I can sit around all day reading encouragements and reflecting but where the rubber meets the road is when I actually take an action as the result of my insights.

I can't wish to be happy, reflect my way into being happy, or demand happiness.

It doesn't work like that.

So, each morning after I'm done reading and reflecting, I remind myself that it's time to get up and get going—start doing the good things that I just considered doing.

It's those activities that will, most likely, make me happy and, hopefully, other people too.

So, I get active. I get going.

Just Go Easy

I remind myself to go easy on the people around me.

I'm hard on myself, so I tend to be hard on others.

But I know that when I pressure people, they are likely to withdraw or snap back at me.

It's only natural.

I react the same way when people pressure me or when I pressure myself.

So, today, I act supportively of the people around me.

I imagine stepping into their shoes and what it's like for them.

As I go easier on them, I'm learning to go easier on myself.

And as I go easier on myself, the people around me respond in kind.

They don't seem as hard on me now as I used to think they were or would be.

Learning to go easy is a great learning process.

It's just not always easy!

Ha!

We're Doing Just Fine

Today, I try not to think poorly of myself.

I stop myself when I'm beginning to belittle or criticize what I'm doing

I do the same with you.

I'll stop myself from being critical of what you're doing.

I think, *Why am I doing that?*

As quickly as I can, I lighten up and laugh.

I think about how I could just as easily be doing the same thing you're doing

So, who am I to judge?

You could just as easily be standing there like me—judging me and laughing at me.

That puts things into perspective and lightens me up even more.

Then I think, if we talk about this, we can do this thing together.

As that old saying goes, *Two heads are better than one.*

If we do that, we'll be doing just fine.

When I Finally Give up

There are moments when I get to the point that I cry out:

"That's it! I give up. I don't want to do this anymore."

What agony I allowed myself to get into by that point.

I just wasn't accepting my limits. I wasn't recognizing how frustrated I had become.

Or, I wasn't admitting that this wasn't my "cup of tea" and I needed to stop.

For whatever reasons, I went beyond my boundaries.

So, I threw up my hands in a tantrum.

I work hard now to stop myself from erupting like that.

When I'm feeling frustrated, I think: Take a break.

I can start again later. I can start again in some other way.

I can talk to someone about it.

Maybe, this is not for me and I'll do something else instead.

But for the moment, I'm done. Time to recoup.

Doing It Your Way

Someone once suggested to me that when things aren't going well, I might just want to try *"doing it the way everybody else is doing it!"*

When he said that, I sarcastically slapped my forehead and responded, *"Wow! Why didn't I think of that?"*

Today, I know that I didn't think of that because I tended to be strong-willed, stubborn, and wanted things "my way."

I know now that many of those old sayings are so true, like:

- when all else fails, read the directions,
- a fool learns from his own mistakes, a wise man learns from everybody else's, and
- Keep It Simple, Sweetheart (KISS it!)

Today, life's a lot easier.

Today, I try to follow directions, doing things the same way everyone else seems to be doing them, and I try to keep it simple.

That works!

Reference Research

The ascribed quotes or paraphrased statements or references attributed to various celebrities, politicians, or well-known historical figures are considered to be in the public domain.

The quote attributed to Mark Twain (page 312) is considered in the public domain. However, in researching this quote, certain scholars at the Center for Mark Twain Studies of Elmira College state they were unable to find "substantial evidence" verifying it as a Mark Twain quote. They note other humorists who have made similar statements, such as, Will Rogers, Kin Hubbard, Artemus Ward, and Josh Billings. See marktwainstudies.com/about and type in the search bar "it ain't what you know."

The expression that Popeye would say (page 320) which I referenced as the English translation of the Hebrew word "YHYH" or "I am what I am" was actually "I yam what I yam." King Features Syndicate, 300 W. 57th St., New York, NY 10019, owns the trademark. The copyright has expired. Note: "Popeye, Grey Owl and Robert Service join the public domain," David MacQuarrie, CBC News, January 12, 2009.

The reference paraphrasing Everett Dirksen (page 354) is considered to be in the public domain and can be referenced at dirksencenter.org. Speeches given by the President and members of Congress are considered to be in the public domain as well as works that are created by the federal government. The quote on the samepage by President John Adams can be found on www.john-adams-heritage.com.

There is a reference to a quote allegedly made by President Theodore Roosevelt (page 311) which is noted on several Internet sites such as: www.brainyquote.com, www.goodreads.com, and www.courthousenews.com, among many other sites, and is also considered to be in the public domain as noted above. The quote attributed to Andrew Carnegie (page 354) can also be found on www.brainyquote.com, as well as numerous other sites.

Some quotation buffs online think that the expression on page 353 about digging yourself into a hole was originated by Will Rogers. However, in contacting the Will Rogers Institute, it was learned that the aphorism cannot be attributed to him.

Every effort has been made to ensure due diligence in researching specific quotes and/or to ascertain that they are considered to be in the public domain. If anything has been omitted or is incorrect, it is unintentional. If notified, the publisher will be pleased to rectify this and include any information in future editions.

Acknowledgments

Nobody writes a book alone.

None of this would have been possible without the help of numerous people who gave of themselves generously, with love, corrections, suggestions, time, and great interest.

First of all, I want to thank two of my children, Gabe and Elyse, for whom I began sending these encouragements two years prior to even thinking about putting them in a book form. Over time, my wife, my sister, and friends became recipients too. Sending these messages to them, having them read them and respond has been a great joy for me. Thanks to all of you.

Randy Levin has been inspirational in his encouragement and information on how to self-publish a book. His guidance and support, as well as humor, have been of great help. Thank you, Randy.

Ellen Marsden has contributed greatly to this book in her review, feedback, grammatical suggestions, and support. I greatly appreciate it. Now get that book of yours published already!

Miriam "Mimi" Schuurmans has also been instrumental in providing insight into how my words can be interpreted differently than I intended. Her perspectives have been invaluable in having me examine what I have written with "fresh eyes." Her grammatical "catches" have been amazing—beating out my other reviewers as well as "Grammarly." Thank you, Mimi.

To my wife, Debbie, who caught so many typos, responded to my encouragement texts with loving GIFs, who has stood by me and encouraged me every step of the way— I love you. And I could not have done it without you. Thank you.

I also need to thank all of the anonymous contributors who have taught me the many lessons in this book and inspire me still today. I have been influenced by such authors as Emmet Fox, Bill Wilson, Rabbi Abraham Twersky, Billy Collins, e.e. cummings, Dorothy Parker, Shel Silverstein, Eve Miriam, and personalities such as Groucho Marx and Yogi Berra, and so many others too numerous to name.

Most of all, as I've written many times in this book, I believe in the tools that have been passed on to me by others, that I practice to the best of my ability every day, and need to be reminded of every day in order to continue to be grateful, to continue to do the best I can, and to support the people not only closest to me but to be as supportive as I can to as many people as I can as I come in contact with them.

And to you who are reading this book, I thank you.

About the Author

Randy Mazie has a Master's of Science in Social Work (MSSW) from Columbia University and a Master's of Business Administration (MBA) from Barry University.

He has worked for a decade with the New York State Office of Mental Health and other social agencies as well as for over thirty years with Miami-Dade County Public Schools.

He has had numerous nonfiction articles published in professional journals, and fiction pieces, short stories as well as poetry, published in such journals as Defenestration, The MacGuffin, The Fredericksburg Literary and Art Review, DASH, Light, The Gyroscope Review, The Orchards Poetry Journal, YourDailyPoem.Com, the Anthology of Transcendent Poetry, Cosmographia Books, 2019, and The Reach of Song Anthology, published by the Georgia Poetry Society, 2021, among other journals and books.

This is his first book in the series: A Year of Encouragements.

Mr. Mazie can be reached at mail@ayearofencouragements.com.

To order books or to learn more about Encouragements, please visit the website at www.ayearofencouragements.com.

A Year of Encouragements is a great gift for family members or friends—for birthdays, special occasions, and to be given to someone as a gift of love who also may need some extra encouragement.

The book is an excellent adjunct for those in the helping professions—psychologists, social workers, doctors, and caregivers—to recommend to their patients to assist them in their continuing desire to independently manage their lives alongside and beyond treatment.

Other items are forthcoming. Please check our website regularly or sign-up for email updates.

We encourage you. ☺

Have you ever been encouraged?

I have!

Made in United States
Orlando, FL
18 January 2022